not just schoolwork

New Directions in Written Expression

by Amy Maid and Roger Wallace

a mandala book

If you need to reproduce the materials in this book, please feel free to do so. As you make additions to the contents we would like to know about them. This helps us to improve on future printings.

If you do reproduce any of the materials please give credit by including the following statement:

Reproduced from . . .

Not Just Schoolwork
Mandala
P.O. Box 796
Amherst, MA 01002

This permission is granted only for reproduction for educational/training events. Permission is not given for large scale-reproduction for sales distribution. If you include a portion of these materials in another publication, please contact us for permission to do so.

MANDALA is an educational and organizational consulting and publishing group. We offer pre- and in-service training courses and workshops in the area of humanistic education, for teachers, nurses, recreational directors, etc. Where people are working with people, we have an interest. Our communication and problem-solving labs and workshops have been attended by people from across the nation. We are especially interested in informing you about these activities. You may receive a current calendar of events by writing to Mandala.

Copyright 1976 by
Mandala
P.O. Box 796
Amherst, MA 01002
First Printing, June, 1976

Library of Congress Catalog Card Number
76-9524
ISBN 0-916250-15-6

Lettering and Illustrations by **AMY MAID**

There are many people who have helped make this book possible. We would like to thank:

Our classes of 1975 and 1976 —
For proving the feasibility of our project

Luke Lennox — our former student —
For suggesting the title

Jacqui and Mareatha Wallace and Barry Maid —
For their encouragement and moral support.

-A.M. & R.W.-

Permissions

table of contents...

INTRODUCTION

In the fifties it was Sputnick that set the stage for America's push toward scientific excellence. The sixties and early seventies spawned the humanistic education movements. This return to the more Dewey progressive-open education was reinforced by the impact of the British primary schools. The middle and later seventies see the slogan "back to the basics" as educationally in. While all three movements are contingent upon political, economical and social attitudes none is sufficient as a sole educational thrust.

Not Just Schoolwork arose out of our needs to provide students with experiences which take into consideration basic needs, human needs, and critical thinking needs. We wanted our students to be able to create expressions that arose out of their experiences in their world. We wanted them to be critical, creative and have the skills to express themselves.

After students are in control of basic writing skills, i.e. sentence structure, paragraphing skills, and creative story writing, it is essential to provide subject matter to write about. Students constantly remark, "I want to write, but what should I write about?" That is when we realized that some relevant curriculum was needed. *Not Just Schoolwork* exists because we value creative thinking, creative writing, social and self awareness.

Not Just Schoolwork is divided into four major sections that focus on the many possibilities of creative thinking.

> I. Perceptions of the World
>
>> Perceiving through the Senses (Do you sense what I sense?)
>> Perceiving the Self (Do you feel what I feel?)
>> Perceiving Others (Do you think what I think?)
>> Perceiving Ideas (Do you see what I see?)
>
> II. Creative Story Writing
>
> III. Units
>
>> Spell and Write
>> Writing the News
>> Holidays
>> Moods
>> Science Fiction
>> Music
>
> IV. Tools of the Trade—helps for student and teacher

HOW TO USE THIS BOOK

Some teachers like to have resources available for students in centers, others organize writing instruction times. Some are informal, others formal in their approach to written expression. It doesn't seem to matter as long as the ultimate goal is to assist the student to mature along the continuum of skill building and expression.

We gave our students weekly writing assignments. The "creative writing" section lends itself to weekly activities. Sections one and three are useable for long or short term assignments. We found that if we did the assignments with our students that their motivation increased. They were interested in our opinions and values and were willing to share theirs as we did ours.

The lessons included here can either be used by teachers as a resource for additional ideas, or can be reproduced as student activity sheets. The activities are not dependent upon each other even though units do exist and can be built upon. As they covered more activities we could begin to blend their expressions with the other subjects we taught. Social Studies and English have many concepts which can be expressed in written form.

TEACHER INPUT

The teacher's role in this program is to assist the student in developing fluency in thinking and writing skills. As facilitator, s/he will provide a student with the opportunity to become open to the world and its complexities. Students will air their values, challenge their stands and make decisions after experimentation. The classroom will become a language arts—social and self awareness laboratory.

We also tried to tie together the cognitive and affective learning processes. We wanted students to differentiate between fact and opinion. We helped them develop options for problem solving. We wanted them to become involved in the process of clarifying their thinking, because they began to think more abstractly. At that point they were able to be involved in the process of thinking about thinking. When students begin to experience their thoughts they are beginning to live this process.

We stressed the mechanics of writing also. However, we tried to nurture our students so that they would not be intimidated by the writing process and perhaps give up. We proceeded slowly and carefully, first allowing the students to become comfortable with their thoughts, then guiding them to begin the technical aspects of correcting and proofreading.

We cannot stress enough that there are no right or wrong answers to our activities. When our students got to the point of believing this, their expression became freer, more fluent and more personally their own.

The final section "Tools of the Trade" is provided so that you can concentrate on skill building. The checklists help students with their verbal expression. The other activities focus on paragraphing, creative story expression and other skills necessary in written expression.

CONCLUSION

When we looked for curriculum materials to help us do what we wanted to do with our students, we found none. This was the first impetus to write this book. Having this book will not solve all your students' creative writing problems. What it will do is to give you and your students a place to start. As your students get past the self consciousness stage, you'll find them using their intuition and imagination. We encourage you in your task of facilitating your students in social and self awareness through written expression, which is **NOT JUST SCHOOLWORK.**

I. perceptions of the world...

Perceiving Through the Senses...

PERCEIVING THROUGH THE SENSES

Have you ever tried to describe some event, object, feeling, or person and found something lacking in your description? We have, and know most people have. Transferring your mental image to written form is difficult. With all your experience, think how difficult that situation would be for your students who are going to write all types of descriptions. You can well imagine that they'll need assistance.

This first section of *Not Just Schoolwork* is designed to ask students to explore and respond to the world with their senses. Each exercise acts as a catalyst to challenge the students to make comparisons, to describe and to identify contrasts. They are then asked to organize, interpret, examine and apply their personal sensory experiences to a written assignment. The exercise lead students to a world they may not have perceived before. Through class discussion and individual conferences with the teacher the students are able to share these observations. By combining these discussions with writing skills, students are growing cognitively and affectively.

Your role in these activities will be to choose appropriate exercises according to the needs of your class. We have not tried to make them developmental in any way. The activities in the beginning are more descriptive while the later ones are more extensive in drawing on the feelings of the students. As discussions and discoveries occur, you can assist the students in the refinement of your thinking. The classroom will become a language-arts sensory awareness laboratory!

The Tools of the Trade section includes the description checklist and feeling checklist. They are tools to be used by the students to give order, to describe characteristics of people, places, objects and feelings. The checklists act as roadmaps which will aid the students in describing phenomena as completely as possible. The checklists can be used again and again according to the needs of your students and the assignments.

As you go through these activities: *ENJOY THEM.* There is a special quality that makes these exercises personal. You will get involved in the lives of your students as they share their excitement in being able to clearly express themselves. You will find that they enjoy hearing from you and the way you perceive with your senses.

This is like homework...

Complete <u>half</u> of the following comparisons. Say whatever comes into your mind.

Spaghetti is like...
My skin is like...
Blue ink is like...
A breeze is like...
A marshmallow is like...
Soda is like...
A tear is like...
A globe is like...
A diamond is like...
Veins are like...
Fire is like

The letter Z is like...
A violin is like...
A submarine is like...
Sneakers are like...
Fear is like...
A clock is like...
A football is like...
Rubber bands are like...
Chocolate cake is like...
A supermarket is like...
A mirror is like...

<u>Hint</u>: Compare each item to something else..."Falling leaves are like silver dollars," "Snow is like vanilla ice cream..."

5

Somewhere over the rainbow...

Complete <u>ten</u> of the following comparisons...the dictionary will help if you are not sure of the colors!

Chartreuse is like...
Amber is like...
Alabaster is like...
Magenta is like...
Sienna is like...
Turquoise is like...

Scarlet is like...
Aqua is like...
Lavender is like...
Ochre is like...
Violet is like...
Beige is like...

Sepia is like...

<u>Hint</u>: Compare each color to something..."Black is like King Kong in an underground cave at midnight," "Red is like a volcano blowing itself apart."

6

dishwasher descriptions...

Choose either #1, #2, or #3.

 **1** Describe a fork in <u>one</u> paragraph. Use your description checklist. Use as many of the five senses as you can. Include <u>DETAILS</u>.

or

 **2** Describe a spoon in <u>one</u> paragraph. Use your description checklist. Use as many of the five senses as you can. Include <u>DETAILS</u>.

or

 **3** Describe a knife in <u>one</u> paragraph. Use your description checklist. Use as many of the five senses as you can. Include <u>DETAILS</u>.

<u>Hint</u>: Put the object you are describing in <u>front</u> <u>of</u> <u>you</u>. You may use comparisons to describe your object.

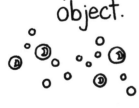  

7

Food for thought...

This is a <u>two</u> paragraph assignment.

1 Describe <u>one</u> of your most <u>favorite</u> foods, in <u>detail</u>. Make it sound incredibly delicious... mouth-watering!

2 Describe <u>one</u> food you really <u>dislike</u>, in <u>detail</u>. Make it sound awful!

<u>Hint</u>: Try to have both foods in front of you while you are writing. Remember to include: sight, smell, sound, texture, and taste.

8

keep on eating...

Sometimes the best part about a meal is in the <u>contrasts</u>... the colors of the foods, textures, the temperatures, and the tastes - sweet, sour, salty...

(1) Plan a <u>full</u> meal using contrasting foods. Example: steaming tomato soup, rare roast beef, mashed potatoes with melted butter, hard rolls, crisp green lettuce, and frosty chocolate ice cream with hot fudge.

(2) <u>Describe</u> a food that you consider "happy" and give your reasons <u>WHY</u>.

(3) Describe a food that you consider "depressing" and give your reasons <u>WHY</u>.

(4) Is caviar a snobbish food? Is chili hot-tempered? Can foods have <u>personalities</u>? Write <u>why</u> or <u>why not</u> and give specific examples to make your point.

know-it-all...

Choose <u>one</u> <u>simple</u> activity (like tying your shoelaces, making a peanut butter sandwich, working a yo-yo, etc.) and <u>describe</u>, in detail, <u>HOW</u> <u>TO</u> <u>DO</u> <u>IT</u>. Your instructions need to be completely accurate so anyone could repeat the activity.

Do the activity yourself - before and during your writing of the instructions - include all steps. Explain even the simplest action.

After completing this assignment give your instructions to someone. Have this person perform the activity by <u>exactly</u> following your instructions.

Did your instructions work? <u>Why</u> or <u>why</u> <u>not</u>?

Color Wheel...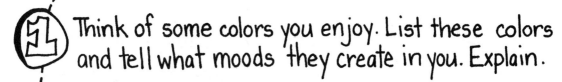

There are colors which reflect the mood of a person. Colors can make a person feel icy cold or lusciously warm. Colors can make people terribly tense, extremely sad, or gleefully happy. A smile can be captured in a gaily colored background and a frown, in a dimly colored room. Color is everywhere!

Answer these questions in <u>three</u> paragraphs:

1. Think of some colors you enjoy. List these colors and tell what moods they create in you. Explain.

2. Write about your <u>angry</u> color. Tell why you feel this way. Write about your <u>snobbish</u> color. Tell why you feel this way. Write about your <u>mysterious</u> color. Tell why you feel this way.

3. With paper and crayons <u>blend</u> some colors (your choice.) How are blended colors different from "plain" colors? Find words to describe how blended colors make you feel.

house beautiful...

Imagine your kitchen pictured in full color in a magazine. Is it the same place without the noises, smells, memories of last night's dinner, and your knowledge of what's in the refrigerator or behind the cupboard doors? In a paragraph (or more) write a description of your kitchen. Make it <u>DETAILED</u>. Include your five senses...sight, sound, smell, touch, and taste. Your description checklist will help you.

<u>Hint</u>: Don't do this from memory. Go into your kitchen, sit down, and write. The reader should have a <u>clear</u> picture in his or her mind of your kitchen from what you write. Rather than naming the sink, stove, and refrigerator, <u>describe</u> them along with the other not as common kitchen equipment or props.

No one ever said it was going to be easy...

Do number one <u>or</u> number two.

1) Describe an apple. (Be sure you have an apple in front of you before you begin.) Try to find other words for <u>red</u> or <u>round</u> in your description. Include your five senses (touch, smell, taste, sight, and sound.) The description checklist is useful here.

2) Describe an egg. (Be sure you have an egg in front of you before you begin.) Try to find other words for <u>white</u>, <u>brown</u>, or <u>oval</u> in your description. Include your five senses (touch, smell, taste, sight, and sound.) The description checklist is useful here.

<u>Hint</u>: This will not be easy to do. You will <u>really</u> have to "look" at your object. Talk about texture, weight, etc. Describe <u>EVERYTHING</u> you see. For example, some apples are not entirely one color. You can compare the object to different things... it smells like, it looks like, etc.

describe...what ?

Have you ever tasted a plan? Or touched a memory? Or seen love? In this activity you will be asked to describe something as difficult.

Choose either #1 or #2. Make your answer one or more paragraphs.

 Describe the taste of water.

or

② Describe the color of your choice to a person who cannot see.

Hint: You will really need to examine your topic...drink a glass of water, look at something that is the color you have chosen. Make your description specific. Use adjectives. You may need to use similes and metaphors.

Teacher: Make lists of similes and metaphors to help your students with them.

14

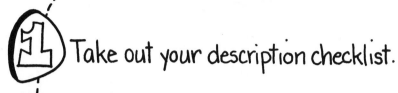

the fort river department store...

1 Take out your description checklist.

2 For your writing assignment today, you will choose <u>one</u> object, found anywhere in the school, to <u>describe</u>, IN DETAIL. Describe the <u>one item you would most like to take home with you</u>! (Maybe you've always dreamed of owning a pay telephone, an electric pencil sharpener, or a coke machine. <u>Before</u> you write - <u>think</u> about all the different things here at school.)

3 Make your description detailed. Go to where the object is and write. Now, in a shorter paragraph, explain <u>WHY</u> you would like to own this thing...what would you do with it, where would you keep it, would you let anyone else use it?

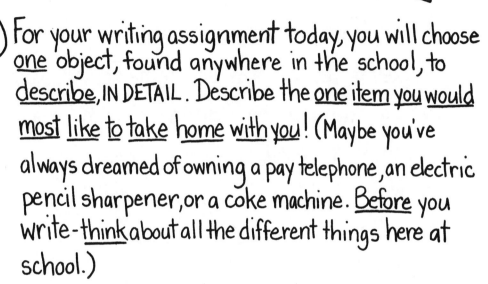

WOW!

listen ... RING RING ZZZ

What does getting up in the morning SOUND like? This will be a description paper - but only sounds. Make the reader hear the same sounds you do when you get up. You can include as much time as you want, up to the time you leave for school. Describe the sounds IN DETAIL. In this description paper, leave out all opinions. This is to be an exact record of the SOUNDS you hear. This should be done in one or more paragraphs. Describe as many sounds as you can.

it's here, somewhere...

Have you ever wondered what a star looks like close up? Do you know what the back of your eyeball feels like? Today we are going to try to find things we

can't see or touch or taste.

Now, make a list of as many things you can think of and answer these questions for _each_ thing you list:

1) If you can't see, touch, or taste this thing, how do you know it exists? ("I just know" isn't enough.)

2) When was the first time (think back) that you "discovered" this thing? What were you doing? What kind of mood were you in?

BUT WHERE IS IT???

a puzzle to ponder...

Which takes up more space... a pickle or a pain?

Paragraph #1... discuss the amount of space a pickle takes up.

Paragraph #2... discuss the amount of space a pain takes up. (You can choose a specific pain, or talk about pain, in general.

Paragraph #3... answer the original question and defend your answer. Explain <u>why</u>. Draw some conclusions.

another puzzle...

Which weighs more...a scream or a sack of potatoes?

Paragraph #1... discuss how much a scream weighs.

Paragraph #2... discuss how much a sack of potatoes weighs.

Paragraph #3... answer the original question and defend your answer. Explain <u>why</u>. Draw some conclusions.

AAAH!!!

POTATO

cold feet...

*Choose one kind of floor!

1 Take off your shoes and socks and feel the floor with your feet. Make a list of eight words (or more) that describe the way the floor feels. (You can stand on carpeting, a wooden floor, linoleum, tile...there are many possibilities.) Be sure to include this list with the rest of the assignment.

2 NOW, use your list of words to describe an object that can be found on Venus. Be sure to name your object and tell what it is used for.

Hint: You can close your eyes to imagine what Venus is like and what objects you'd find there.

beauty is in the eye of the beholder...

In this writing assignment you will write about the most beautiful things you can think of. These can be particular things, actions, feelings, or moods. Your essay will be five paragraphs long:

Paragraph #1... define beauty. What does it mean to you?

Paragraph #2... describe something that you think is beautiful. (IN DETAIL). Why do you think this thing is beautiful?

Paragraph #3... describe a second thing that you think is beautiful. (IN DETAIL). Why do you think this thing is beautiful?

Paragraph #4... describe a third thing that you think is beautiful. (IN DETAIL). Why do you think this thing is beautiful?

Paragraph #5... it is often said that "Beauty is in the eye of the beholder." What do you think this means?

Hint: Describe beauty by using colorful adjectives, detailed descriptions, metaphors, and similes.

Perceiving the Self...
(Do you feel what I feel?)

PERCEIVING THE SELF

"I celebrate myself and sing myself . . . ."
—Walt Whitman

Students need an opportunity to define and explain themselves. This section was developed to allow your students that opportunity. In it they gather information from their own experience, bodies and feelings.

Each exercise provides a frame of reference to initiate thought. From that point the students must define, translate and interpret a relationship between the concepts in the assignment and themselves. The students are responsible for analyzing and evaluating their own values and opinions. The final product may be a thought provoking paragraph, thoughtfully answered questions, stimulating discussion or an autobiography.

In order for your students to reach higher thought levels it is necessary to provoke precise responses from them. We found that most students gave general answers. We had to say things like "Why" or "How come" in order to get them to be more specific. The more we pushed for preciseness the more they reached for higher levels of expression.

Part of the self is examining the choices one makes. In most of the assignments in this section students make choices or decide on points of view. Once students decide where they stand on an issue they need to be fluent in the description which demonstrates their choice. The defense of the position is important as well as the point of view.

Ultimately we are concerned that students internalize their values, have a positive sense of self and experience their sense of competence. As we saw them and listened to them share their work we become more convinced that our goals for self awareness and growth were happening to them and us.

forget it ...remember it

Spend some time thinking and making a list of the things you'd like to forget or remember.

Then describe one thing you'd most like to forget or remember. Write <u>WHY</u> you would like to forget it or remember it.

(This can be a person, a bad experience, a good experience... ANYTHING!)

i seem to be a verb...

Think about the different parts of speech: nouns, verbs, adjectives, pronouns, adverbs, prepositions, conjunctions, and interjections. Which part of speech are <u>you</u> most like...and <u>WHY</u>? First, think about what each part of speech <u>is</u> and <u>does</u>. Then, think about what <u>you</u> are like. Make some comparisons. Write your answer in a paragraph.

who, me ?

You're like many <u>things</u>. You look like things and you act like things. Pick <u>one</u> of these things and compare yourself to it.

In one paragraph (or more) write <u>how</u> you are like the thing you have chosen. Try to be specific: if you are comparing yourself to a car, make sure you mention what kind of car you are like...Porsche, Cadillac, Toyota, etc. If you are comparing yourself to a tree, mention the kind of tree...birch, elm, Christmas, redwood, etc.

<u>Ideas</u>: to compare yourself to...food, furniture, clothing, appliances, tools...

Self-portraits...

1 Draw a picture representing <u>your</u>: **id, ego, and super ego.** (<u>Three</u> pictures, one for <u>each</u>.)

Things to consider: What is each one — <u>define</u> id, ego, and super ego. What does <u>your</u> id, ego, and super ego <u>do</u> for <u>you</u>?

2 Now, write several paragraphs to <u>explain</u> what you have drawn. Try to explain everything in your pictures.

<u>Teacher</u>: This assignment was done after a class discussion of id, ego, and super ego.

and, for only $49.95...

Companies are always coming out with new and improved versions of their products. Some have new flavors or new scents, or more power and zip. If you could be redesigned and repackaged, how would you be new and improved? Consider your looks and/or your personality. Write a paragraph and draw a picture of your NEW YOU.

A NEW ME ???

... and who are you?

"i-i hardly know, just at present - at least i know who i was when i got up this morning, but i think i must have been changed several times since then."
— Lewis Carroll

Write a paragraph about how <u>you</u> have changed since morning - this morning or any other morning... Have someone else write a paragraph on how you have changed since this morning.

30

madison avenue...

BOLD, EXCITING, REFRESHING...

Advertisements are everywhere...television, radio, magazines, billboards, stores, newspapers, subways... People also advertise themselves! Look at the people around you - the way they look tells you something about them. Blue jeans, a policeman's uniform, and a suit and tie suggest a difference in what people are doing, and perhaps, in their personalities.

1. List as many ways you can think of on how you advertise yourself. <u>Why</u> have you chosen to present this information about you to other people?

2. What's hard to tell about a person from the way he or she looks?

3. Why do <u>you</u> think people form opinions about a person from the way he or she looks? Think of when you have done this. Try to form an opinion without "trying the product."

4. What do you think people hope to gain by advertising themselves in a certain way? Explain.

the 10-most wanted list...

YOU have been missing for three months. A member of the Missing Persons Bureau is looking for you. (Agent 006.) Describe the person Agent 006 is looking for:

Paragraph #1... Invent a reason why you are missing.

Paragraph #2... Describe your physical appearance in detail. (Use your description checklist.) Do you have any unusual or identifying features? If so, describe. What clothes are you most likely to be wearing? Describe.

Paragraph #3... What habits do you have that might help Agent 006 recognize you? Describe three or four habits.

Paragraph #4... To what places (specific or general) are you likely to go? Describe.

Paragraph #5... What things are you likely to do while you are missing? Describe.

Paragraph #6... What people (be specific) are you likely to get in touch with while you are missing? Why these particular people?

Remember, while you are "on the road" you will have to eat and sleep. You will be doing something, somewhere, each day. Where are you most likely to be, eat, sleep, etc?

my way...

Inside myself I feel feelings like everyone else. When I stand in front of a mirror I look like no one else. My fingerprints are different. My face is different. I walk differently. I talk differently.

While all of us can do things that are similar - like sports, writing, hobbies, being a son or daughter, there are special things that are unique. Consider how you laugh, what you feel, the way you treat others. What's your special touch that makes you different?

 1 In what ways are <u>you</u> different?

 2 <u>Why</u> are you different in these ways?

 3 When is being different a help and when is it a handicap?

take pride...

Everyone has at least <u>one</u> thing that they do well. In a paragraph broadcast to the world about your talent. Be sure to include <u>what</u> you do well, <u>how</u> you learned to do it, if you practice, and <u>why</u> you think you do it well. In your paragraph include the feelings you have about possessing this talent.

dreams or nightmares...

It has been said that... "Yesterday's dreams are a small pile of ashes."

1 What do you think this quotation means? Explain and analyze.

2 Explain some of your dreams that didn't work out or really don't mean too much anymore.

3 When does a dream become a nightmare? Explain.

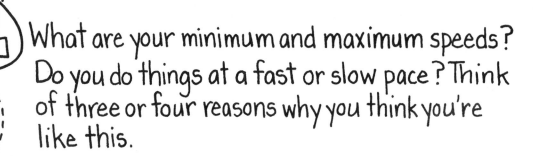

maximum speed: 55 miles per hour

1) What are your minimum and maximum speeds? Do you do things at a fast or slow pace? Think of three or four reasons why you think you're like this.

2) Write how doing things <u>fast</u> can help you <u>and</u> hurt you.

3) Write how doing things <u>slowly</u> can help <u>and</u> hurt you.

<u>Hint</u>: When writing how going fast can help or hurt you consider things like: taking risks, being responsible, being a leader or follower, being vulnerable...

day dream...

Plan <u>two</u> perfect days for yourself. Start with the time you get up until the time you go to sleep. What will you do, where will you go, will you be with anybody, what and where will you eat, will you buy anything (if so, what), will you see anything "special?" <u>Why</u> do you want to do these things? Plan each day in a separate paragraph. Don't worry about money or transportation, but be realistic in terms of what you can do in one day.

inside out... ?

Many times when you feel things getting on your nerves, you aren't reacting to those things - instead, you are reacting to something <u>inside</u> of you. Many times these reactions "inside" are worse than the situation itself.

1 Think of the words <u>you say to yourself</u> when you are unhappy about the way people are treating you? Why do you think you say these things?

2 What are the sentences <u>you hear in your head</u> when you try to overcome a difficult problem? Why do you think these sentences are there?

3 What do <u>you see yourself doing</u> when people around you are angry and are acting mean? Why do you think you do what you do?

4 What are the <u>thoughts you have</u> when you feel tired but have <u>not</u> yet reached your goal? Why do you think what you do?

5 What do <u>you say to yourself</u> when people around you are treating others unfairly? Why do you think you say these things?

do it...

Interview ten people to find out what they would like to be sure to accomplish before they die. From that list or from ideas of your own, what would <u>you</u> like to do before you die? Think of <u>why</u> you want to do this thing so badly. Write a paragraph explaining your choice.

me, myself, and i ...

This is a project for the week... an <u>AUTOBIOGRAPHY</u>.

Paragraph #1... <u>Birth Facts</u>: Time, where, date, name of hospital. Were you named after anyone - who? Why did your parents name you what they did? Include your middle name. Birth weight, height. Include any other interesting facts about your birth. What is your birth sign?

Paragraph #2... <u>Family</u> & <u>Home</u>: Describe <u>each</u> member of your family so people will know what they are like - looks, personality, occupation, age. Where do you fit - oldest, middle, youngest? Any famous relatives? What ethnic group is your family? Do you have any pets - if so, what kind, names, how long have you had them? Describe the house you live in now. Where else have you lived - other cities, other houses? How old were you when you moved? What do you remember about these places? Include anything else that is interesting about your family or your background. (Hobbies, family projects, etc.)

Me, myself, and i ...

Paragraph #3... <u>Early</u> <u>Life</u> (ages 1-6) and

Paragraph #4... <u>Later</u> <u>Life</u> (ages 7-present): Describe things you remember that happened to you in your life during these two time periods. Do this <u>in order</u> – people you met, things you did, places you went to, events both sad and happy. You can also use stories that your parents have told you, especially ages 1-6.

Paragraph #5... <u>Memorable</u> <u>Events</u>: Talk about important things that have happened to you in your life... birthdays, beginning school, getting a pet, moving-ANYTHING you consider important in your life. (Your feeling checklist will help you.) Be sure to include one of the <u>best</u> things that ever happened to you and one of the <u>worst</u> things that ever happened to you, and explain <u>WHY</u>.

me, myself, and i ...

I LIKE...

Paragraph #6... <u>Description</u> of <u>You</u> as <u>You</u> <u>are</u> <u>Now</u>: What do you look like (describe in detail), what is your personality like (shy, out-going, athletic, sensitive, etc.?) What are your faults? What are your interests, hobbies, habits? Do you belong to any clubs or organizations? Have you ever won an award? How have you changed in the last year? <u>WHAT</u> <u>MAKES</u> <u>YOU</u>, <u>YOU</u>? You can include what others say about you. (One way to complete this part of your project is to have some of your friends interview you. Have a tape recorder running so you can transcribe what you say. Topics for the interview could include your views on: politics, religion, money, work, sex roles, etc.)

Paragraph #7... <u>Likes</u> <u>and</u> <u>Dislikes</u>: What are some of your favorites- color, food, T.V. show, song, book that you've read, season, etc? Who do you admire, famous and non-famous people? What is your idea of having a good time? What do you find boring? What do you dislike? Include any other likes and dislikes

me, myself, and i...

you can think of. What are your pet peeves? What is something you get angry about?

Paragraph #8... <u>Feelings</u>: What are some things you feel strongly about? What is <u>important</u> to you? Why are these things important to you? Explain. Choose some words from the feeling checklist to help you describe feelings which are descriptions of you.

Paragraph #9... <u>Others</u>: How do you think <u>other</u> people see <u>you</u>? Describe and explain why you think people see you the way they do. What do you think people think of you?

Paragraph #10... <u>Future Plans</u>: Discuss your hopes for the future - career, education, accomplishments, possessions you hope to have, family plans, where you hope to live, what you would like to be doing, travel, etc. Include anything else you are planning for the future - dreams, wishes, ambitions...

<u>Teacher</u>: Students were told that any information they considered too sensitive to discuss could be omitted from their autobiographies. They were also encouraged to make this a multi media project.

43

money, the minute you want it...

What <u>two</u> things would you <u>most</u> like money for:

to do things for other people ?

to fulfill a dream of yours?

to be able to go wherever you want ?

to feel grown-up ?"

to buy your own food and clothing ?

why? Be specific. Write a paragraph explaining your choices.

Save it for a rainy day...

Imagine that you are going to pack <u>three</u> of your possessions away in a trunk that you will <u>not</u> open for fifty years...

What three things will you put away and <u>WHY</u>?

Consider what you will want to see from your childhood things. Also, think about <u>why</u> people save things...memories, because they will become valuable with time, etc. The items you choose must be in your possession <u>now</u>.

Write three paragraphs. In each one, <u>name</u> the item you will save, <u>describe</u> it, and give your reasons <u>why</u> it is important to you to save it.

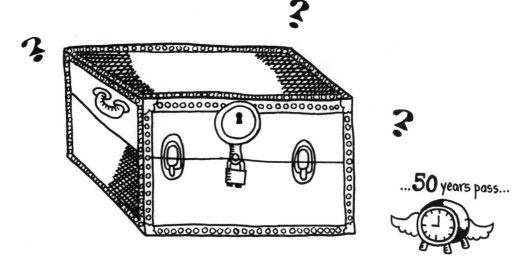

...50 years pass...

45

So Long...

If you were forced to leave your home and pack all your possessions in only <u>one</u> suitcase (medium size), <u>what</u> things would you take along, and <u>why</u> would you take them? These must be things you can pack in a suitcase. Think about things that really mean a lot to you, things that you wouldn't want to lose. Make your answer a paragraph long.

I'D TAKE MY...

i'd rather be...

Which would you rather be...

an only child ?

the youngest child ?

the oldest child ?

 why ?

Write a paragraph explaining your choice.

MINE ooo

What do you mean when you say that an object "belongs to you..?" There are obvious answers such as: "I paid for it," "Someone gave it to me," or "I have a piece of paper that says it's mine." Try to think of others.

What is the RELATIONSHIP between you and the thing? What does it mean to you, and what do you mean to it?

A thing might be valued because it performs a useful service, like a warm coat, or a pair of ice skates. It might have value because it is a symbol of success, like a trophy, or a diploma. Or it might have value because of the memories it represents, like a childhood toy, or a photograph.

1. Choose one of your most valued possessions (make it an object.) Write a paragraph, or more, about how much this possession means to you. Describe the object. Explain how you acquired it. Why is it so valuable to you?

2. Now, write another paragraph which expresses the opposite feeling. Pretend that you dislike this possession (the same object you wrote about in the first paragraph) and try to be convincing, so it seems you really don't like it. Do not make up things about the object that are not true. Find things which would make you feel opposite toward the object.

luck or skill ...

Some things in life happen because of <u>luck</u>, and other things happen because of <u>skill</u>.

1   Write a paragraph about something that has happened to you because of some <u>skill</u> you possess. This can be something you got to do, something you are able to do, or something that happened to you... but only because of some special talent or skill that you have.

2   Write a paragraph about something that has happened to you, something you got to do, or something you are able to do because you are <u>lucky</u>. Remember, this example must be due to luck, only.

3   Life is made up of skill and luck. Try to explain the different importance of each. Point out how both can be used to your advantage. Make several lists of times when luck and skill works.

back when...

Look around the room at different people or things until you see something that reminds you of something from your past — a place, person, an object, or event. Write that memory. That memory can now help you think of other things. Once you get started, keep going. Don't worry about the order of things. Let your thoughts flow through your head. It may help to close your eyes when you do this. Now answer these questions:

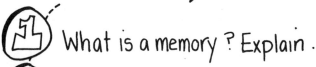

1. What is a memory? Explain.

2. How do your memories make you feel? Discuss.

3. Why do you think that you remember only certain things and forget other things?

4. What does it mean to "live on memories alone?"

5. Find five or six reasons why memories are good things.

do you believe...

I THINK... ? ?

(1) List about five things you believe in strongly. Explain your feelings about these things. Did you consider things like family, religion, and money?

(2) What are some issues on which you have <u>not</u> yet formed a definite opinion? Tell why you haven't made your mind up and the pro's and con's of the issue. Consider things like drugs, life and friendship.

(3) Have you ever made a choice that surprised everyone? What was it and <u>why</u>? If not, why do you think your decisions are so predictable?

GEE, I DON'T KNOW...

a pot of gold...

It is said that at the end of every rainbow there is a pot of gold which will bring the person who finds it good luck and wealth. You now have your own personal rainbow...

1. What is at the end of it? (Think in terms of your GOALS and AMBITIONS.)

2. How will you get to it? (How will you reach your goals, what will you have to do?)

3. What obstacles might you encounter along the way?

4. What are some things you might have to do without, or sacrifice, because of your rainbow?

5. Will anyone else benefit from your "pot of gold?" Why or why not?

6. Why is your "pot of gold" so important to you?

This essay is a look at the goals you have set for yourself. They can change. You may use short-term goals (one or two days away), or long-term goals set far in the future.

Write one paragraph for each question.

growing up... Time Flies...

What is the difference between you and adulthood?
Do this assignment in two paragraphs – one paragraph
explaining the differences, and one paragraph stating
your conclusions about the differences.

? ? ? ? ? ? ? ? ? ?   WELL, I'M...

---

yes and no...

Try to list the times you say "yes" and the times
you say "no". Do you find anything in common in
your lists.

How would your life be different (or would it be) if you
said "no" instead of "yes" much more often? Answer
this question in a paragraph. Be sure to use specific examples,
and talk about the consequences of this action – saying "no" to
most things.   NO!   YES!

the cold shoulder...

"People always turned their backs on me. Nobody ever bothered to speak to me kindly. While groups of people would play together, I would always play alone or stand in a corner, watching them. It wasn't that I was afraid of them, I just didn't know what to say.

As I grew older, being alone became a bigger problem. I had no one to go to baseball games with. Every time I went to the movies, I went alone. It's a lonely feeling when you live like that.

I figured out that I couldn't live that way. So I went out and tried to meet people. I found out that I could talk to someone if I tried to be honest. I decided that I wasted too much time being alone. If I had made an effort to reach people, they would have reached out and greeted me..."

1. What do _you_ think was this person's problem? Explain.

2. How would _you_ handle this problem? Explain.

3. Think of times you have a problem speaking to people. Do any of those times have anything in common?

4. When do _you_ turn your back on people? Describe what _honesty_ has to do with communicating with people.

54

to have or not to have...

These are qualities that a person may have. Number the list below (1-15) in order of their importance to you.

popularity

sophistication

sensitivity

being trusted

honesty

helpfulness

creativity

uniqueness

athletic ability

sense of humor

pride

intelligence

being brave

talent

level-headed

Now, write a paragraph on why your #1 choice is the most important to you, and write a paragraph on why your #15 choice is last on your list. Take some time to compare your choices and reasons with each other.

<u>Teacher</u>: Process this lesson by asking your students to fill in the blanks:

I learned...   I wish...   I hope...

I was surprised...   I want...

who do you trust?

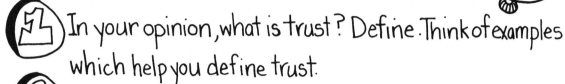

1. In your opinion, what is trust? Define. Think of examples which help you define trust.

2. Why do you trust someone? Explain. Think of the characteristics of people you trust.

3. Who do you trust? Make a list. (Family, friends, teachers, etc.)

4. People are either born with distrust or they learn it. Which do you think happens? Do you have anything to prove your answer?

5. In your opinion, how important is it to be able to trust someone? Explain.

6. How long does it take you to know if you can trust someone or not - 20 minutes, 2 hours, 2 days - which one is most like you?

7. What are the things about you that convince others you can be trusted?

8. In your opinion, at what stage in a person's life does trust develop?

protect yourself...

During the course of a day, you sometimes find yourself in situations where you can be hurt physically - many times those type of accidents can be avoided. But how do you protect yourself from the personal hurts you feel inside - hurt feelings, hurting others, feeling impatient, left-out, etc.? Answer these questions in several paragraphs.

TO PROTECT YOURSELF FROM PERSONAL HURTS:

 How do you act? Explain.

 What do you say to yourself? Explain.

 What do you do about the situation? Explain.

 How is the future different because of your actions?

Calling Outer Space...

If life does exist on another planet or in space, I wonder why they haven't bothered to make contact with humans. I have a couple of good reasons why they might <u>never</u> try to reach us. People of different nations are at war constantly. People of different colors are always fighting over their rights. People steal, people kill, people hate! Given a choice, would you want to introduce yourself to this?

In a paragraph (or more) explain <u>why</u> you think people on earth fight, declare war, commit crimes, and generally treat each other poorly.

HELLO?

happy birthday...

Which would <u>you</u> rather have your friend give you for your birthday...

    ... a gift your friend picks out?

    ... money to buy yourself something?

    ... a gift that your friend makes for you?

    ... nothing but good wishes?

In a paragraph, explain your choice. Now, rank order the four items. Which would you choose second, third, and fourth? Share your list with another person. How are your choices similar or different?

alone in a crowd...

"Friends are really strange - well, at least mine are! We do the regular things, tell secrets, play together, and fight for each other. The problem is that my friends expect me to do all the things that they do. They say, 'If you are our friend, you'll do such and such.' How do I make them understand that there are things I just <u>WON'T</u> do?"

 Why do <u>you</u> think this problem sometimes occurs? Explain.

 What would <u>your</u> solution to this problem be? Explain.

 What do you think "being alone in a crowd" means? Discuss. Do you agree this can happen? Why or why not?

60

me and you and a dog named blue...

Imagine that you are shipwrecked on a deserted island. You may pick any <u>three</u> people (or animals) that you would like with you on the island. Write a paragraph for each person or animal that you picked. Include: who, why, what you expect from them, what you can provide for them.

The people you choose may be friends, acquaintances, famous people, etc.

Friendship...

1 What two qualities do you <u>most</u> want in a friend?

2 Name <u>three</u> ways in which a present friendship of yours would be better, if only the other person would...

3 What did <u>you</u> do and/or say to yourself the last time a friend disappointed you? <u>Why</u> did you react that way?

4 Which do you think is harder for you - to <u>make</u> a friend or <u>keep</u> a friend? Why?

Answer each question in a paragraph.

Thank you, mr. edison...

"I'm always trying to do something outstanding. Every time that I do something I find out that it has already been done."

Write a paragraph that explains something <u>new</u> you could do. Explain this activity in detail. Now answer these questions:

1) Describe the importance of doing something that has <u>never</u> been done before.

2) How can <u>you</u> benefit from doing things that have been done before?

3) Describe the creative person. Then describe yourself. See how your two descriptions are similar.

4) People who are extremely creative and inventive are sometimes <u>not</u> recognized, and are even persecuted by the society in which they live. They are often labeled "quacks". Their genius is not recognized until many years later - many times after the person has died. What would <u>you</u> do if you did something truely brilliant and no one would listen to you? What would be the things that would keep you at work in spite of public ridicule? What would make you want to quit and conform to society?

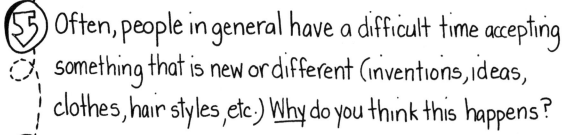

thank you, mr. edison...?

5) Often, people in general have a difficult time accepting something that is new or different (inventions, ideas, clothes, hair styles, etc.) <u>Why</u> do you think this happens?

6) What is the last "different" thing you wanted to do that you were <u>serious</u> about, and you met with disapproval from your parents, teachers, friends or anyone else? <u>Why</u> do you think this happened?

Perceiving Others...

(Do you think what I think?)

PERCEIVING OTHERS

Students are affected by peers, teachers, custodial and transportation staff. They reshape their views of life as others surround them. This section focuses students on the people around them. It is designed for them to interpret, analyze and evaluate the way they view relationships. It is a look at human interaction and the people process.

When our students began to think of others they realized that their lives were filled with information about others. Personal relationships, trust and peer pressure were some of the things which arose. We've used these concepts in our activities. These topics stimulated discussion of the actual events in their lives.

One student who was promoted to Junior High returned to explain that although she had not taken the assignments seriously, she could now see how they applied to her life. We talked about changes in her social environment and how those changes really affect the way she felt about those around her.

The students developed their own Hall of Fame. They were gracious with their honors. They named mothers, fathers, friends, relatives and a variety of others, whom they perceived as famous. Their reason for choosing particular people was quite clear. They identified people who made some significant contribution in their lives.

film...

"I am a camera. You are a camera. Perhaps I am in your movie. Perhaps you are in mine. Perhaps a film festival is in order. We could all share our scenes..."

Develop <u>your</u> film. Who do you share your scenes with and <u>how</u> do you share them? Answer this questions in several paragraphs.

---

president for a day...

If <u>you</u> were the President of the United States, which would you spend the <u>most</u> money on... and why?

... the Space Program   ...the National Defense Program

... the Poverty Program   ...Reconstruction of Inner Cities

... Foreign Aid   ... Educational Reform

Which would you spend the <u>least</u> on? why?

pro or con...

With another person take <u>one</u> side of argument. Persuade your audience that:

1. Girls should (or should not) be allowed to play Little League Baseball.

   <u>or</u>

2. All students should (or should not) be allowed to use calculators while doing math.

Choose #1 or #2. Decide if you are for (pro) or against (con) the statement. Have good, solid reasons to back up your point of view. "Because" is inadequate. Think of <u>all</u> the reasons you can. (This may be easier to do if you pretend you are having an argument with someone.) You will both have a chance to present your point of view.

fame...

Who would you place in your <u>own</u> personal Hall of Fame?
Think of <u>five</u> people (famous <u>and</u> non-famous) to induct into your
Hall of Fame. Explain <u>why</u> these people deserve to be recognized
(what they have done.) Try not to pick more than one person from
the same occupation. This is a five-paragraph assignment.

---

you and me...

"There is no one who knows everything; there is no one
who knows nothing."

1) What do <u>you</u> think this quotation means? Explain.

2) Do you agree with it? Why or why not?

3) What is something <u>you</u> would like to learn from
someone else?

4) What is something <u>you</u> would like to teach?

tea for two...

Choose <u>seven</u> <u>famous</u> people with whom you would like to have dinner. Start with Sunday and write <u>one</u> paragraph for <u>each</u> day of the week... write <u>who</u> you would like to have to dinner and <u>why</u> <u>you</u> <u>would</u> <u>like</u> <u>to</u> <u>have</u> <u>dinner</u> <u>with</u> <u>that</u> <u>person</u>. Write why you think that person is interesting. What do you expect to learn <u>about</u> that person? What do you want to learn <u>from</u> that person? What will that person learn from <u>you</u>? What will you talk about?

Try <u>not</u> to choose people in the same occupation. Be sure to include where you would eat and what you would order.

the choice of a lifetime...

If it was possible to choose <u>one</u> thing for <u>all</u> the people living in this country, would you choose to:

1- make <u>all</u> the people <u>rich</u> (millionaires)?

2- make <u>all</u> the people <u>honest</u>?

3- make <u>all</u> the people <u>healthy</u>?

4- make <u>all</u> the people <u>young</u>?

Answer this question and write <u>why</u> you feel the way you do. Do this assignment in several paragraphs.

do unto others...

"There is a destiny that makes us brothers...none goes his way alone. All that we send into the lives of others...comes back into our own." — E. Markham

1 Describe what this quote means to you.

2 With what do you agree or disagree? Write a paragraph discussing your feelings and ideas about this statement. The feeling checklist will help you.

---

heavy...

"I do my thing, and you do your thing.
I am not in this world to live up to your expectations.
And you are not in this world to live up to mine.
You are you and I am I.
And if by chance we find each other, it's beautiful.
If not, it can't be helped." — Frederick Perls

1 What is Frederick Perls saying to you in this quote. Explain in a paragraph.

2 React to the meaning of the last line. Check the feeling checklist to express your feelings fully.

72

the grass is always greener...

"...i cried because i had no shoes until i met a man who had no feet..."

Your writing assignment is to analyze this statement.

A Guideline

Paragraph #1... What do you think this proverb means?

Paragraph #2... Why do you think people are sometimes dissatisfied with themselves, their lives, and what they have?

Paragraph #3... Does this proverb have any meaning in your life? Give some examples of how it does or doesn't.

Paragraph #4... Is being dissatisfied the same as being selfish? Is it the same as being greedy? What words would you use in place of "dissatisfied?"

Paragraph #5... How does a person choose between what they really need and what they want? What kinds of things do you really need, and what things do you just think you need, but could live without? Be specific.

Paragraph #6... What is the general attitude or message this proverb communicates? How does it make you feel?

73

Perceiving Ideas...
(Do you see what I see?)

PERCEIVING IDEAS

All that exists in the world is identified through ideas. The tree that stands outside your home, the quiet person in a noisy crowd, the picking of proper clothes, all deal with perceiving ideas we have about them. The exercises in this section ask the students to examine, react, analyze and evaluate the many ideas of the world. Some of the exercises focus on areas such as: origins of particular assumptions, capital punishment and the inevitability of change. The objective of this section is to have the students open up to the world's ideas.

This section led to many discussions and much thoughtful writing. Our students' conversations were self-examining, and thorough in that they encompassed identification and evaluation of the issues. The writing levels were expanded because the subject matter forced the students to use examples or give proof of why certain ideas exist as they do.

The exercises, like the previous ones, allow the students opportunities to shape and reshape different ideas. The quotations in this section were included to guide the student to some basic concepts that are a part of our world. Through the use of the quotations, poems, and general statements, we hope you look beyond the assignments to the values the students must exhibit through their answers.

think about it...

1. What is an idea? Explain.

2. What makes people have _different_ ideas?

3. How do people get _NEW_ ideas?

4. How do _you_ get an idea?

5. When and where do _you_ get ideas? (Most often.)

6. What kind of _mood_ do you have to be in to get an idea?

7. Write one idea that _you_ have had (about anything.)

8. Some people think that there is nothing new in the world—everything has already been done and invented. React.

Write some ideas about:

soundproof...

If a tree falls in a forest and there is _no one_ there, does the tree make a sound? _THINK_-try to reason this out.

Answer the question and explain _why_ you came to your decision.

a story without words...

Several years ago there was a well-known advertisement for a camera company which featured the slogan: "One picture is worth a thousand words."

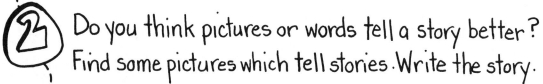

1 What do you think this slogan means?

2 Do you think pictures or words tell a story better? Find some pictures which tell stories. Write the story.

3 If words tell stories better, <u>why</u> do <u>you</u> people paint or take photographs? What are the benefits of doing something <u>visually</u>? What are the disadvantages?

4 If pictures tell stories better, <u>why</u> do <u>you</u> think people write books, poetry, drama? What are the advantages of doing something in <u>printed</u> form? What are the disadvantages?

Answer <u>each</u> question in a paragraph.

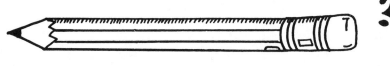

why?

Write <u>one</u> question beginning with the word "<u>WHY</u>" and then answer it in <u>one</u> paragraph or more.

<u>Ideas</u>: <u>Why</u> is the sky blue?

<u>Why</u> do people hurt each other?

<u>Why</u> is Hank Aaron such a good home-run hitter?

<u>Why</u> does McDonalds make so much money?

etc.

* Be sure to write the question you are answering!

<u>Teacher</u>: This assignment can be expanded to include:

Write one question beginning with the word "<u>WHO</u>."
Write one question beginning with the word "<u>HOW</u>."
Write one question beginning with the word "<u>WHAT</u>."
Write one question beginning with the word "<u>WHERE</u>."
Write one question beginning with the word "<u>WHEN</u>."

79

the payment: pro or con...

Adults get paid for the work they do. So it seems only fair that kids should get paid for the work they do — going to school!

1. First, argue **for** this statement. Give **all** your reasons why kids should be paid for the work they do in school. Be convincing!

2. Now, take the **opposite** point of view and argue **against** this statement. Give **all** your reasons why kids should **not** be paid for the work they do in school. Again, be convincing.

Answer these questions fully with examples.

---

junk...

1. Make a list of **ten** or more things that **you** think are junk.

2. Where do you find junk?

3. Some people collect junk. Write a paragraph or more about a piece of junk you have collected and can't bear to get rid of.

4. "The mind is really a junkyard." What do **you** think that means? Do you agree with it? Why or why not?

JUNK?

do you see what i see?

1. Do you think you see the world differently than your parents, or your teachers, or your friends? Explain.

2. Pick <u>one</u> thing or idea that you think you look at differently than other people. In your <u>first</u> paragraph, write about how <u>you</u> look at the thing or idea you picked. Now, try to put yourself in someone else's place...one of your teachers, parents, or friends, and write a <u>second</u> paragraph about how you think that person sees the <u>same</u> <u>thing</u> you do.

   <u>Ideas</u> <u>you</u> <u>might</u> <u>want</u> <u>to</u> <u>consider</u>: a T.V. show, honesty, politics, a book, spending money, the time you go to sleep, eating a certain food...

3. Add a paragraph which describes your feelings about these differences. Your feeling checklist will help you.

life...

"Too much sanity may be madness and the maddest of all, is to see life as it is and not as it should be."
— Man of La Mancha

Do you agree with this statement... that it is <u>better</u> to have dreams of what <u>could</u> be, than to see life as it really <u>is</u> today? Answer this question and write why or why not. Do this in a paragraph.

Make a list of feelings this quote causes in you. Pick some of these feelings to be described in a paragraph.

---

an impossible assignment...

Write several paragraphs about an impossible relationship that you would like to have happen. For example: you and Robert Redford, snow on a 95° day, the Boston Red Sox winning the Super Bowl.

In your paragraphs answer these questions:

1. <u>What</u> is the impossible relationship?

2. <u>Why</u> would you like the relationship to happen?

3. <u>Why</u> will this relationship <u>NEVER</u> take place?

THIS IS IMPOSSIBLE!

One person's treasure is another person's junk...

Think of something you own that you value highly and that someone else might consider "junk." Or, think about something that someone else owns that they think is valuable and that you consider "junk." Name the object and write:

Paragraph #1... Why do you think of the object the way in which you do? In other words, why do you consider it either valuable or junk?

Paragraph #2... Why do you think that the other person (be specific, name a person) considers the object valuable or junk?

a fish story...

"If you give me a fish, I will eat tonight. If you teach me how to fish, I will eat for a lifetime." — CHINESE PROVERB

1. What do you think this quotation means? Explain.
2. How does it apply to you?
3. What is operating in this quote - id, ego, or super ego? Why? Defend your point.

Teacher: This lesson was done after a discussion of id, ego, and super ego.

---

the winning answer...

1. How do you feel about a person who always plays to win? Why do you feel this way?
2. When, if ever, is winning NOT important?
3. Why do you think people want to win? How do you deal with winning and losing - what do you say, what do you do?
4. Is losing ever good? Why or why not?

Answer all these questions - a paragraph for each. Use examples.

Social Climbing...

"Some people reach the top of the ladder only to find that it is leaning against the wrong wall."

1) What do _you_ think this quotation means?

2) What do _you_ think it means to "reach the top of the ladder?"

3) Why do _you_ think there is so much importance in this country placed on achievement, social climbing, getting up the ladder of success, and "keeping up with the Joneses?"

4) How are "getting ahead" and "achievement" important? If you think success is important, explain _why_. If you think it is unimportant, explain _why_.

5) Is success _always_ a good thing? Why or why not?

6) Why do you think "failure" is considered a bad thing? Is it bad? Why or why not?

7) How do _you_ handle failure? What do you do, say to yourself, how do you act?

GOING UP!

in the beginning...

Imagine that when a baby is born s/he is able to understand whatever you say. In several paragraphs, write what you feel the baby should know about dealing with life. In other words, give your <u>best</u> advice to an infant on how to survive in <u>this</u> <u>world</u>.

Consider sharing things like: how to make money, how to get along with others, how to be part of a family, how to get what you want, how to be happy...

wandering...

"If sometimes you don't get lost, there's a chance you may <u>never</u> find your way."

1° In your opinion, what do you think the quote means?

2° Do you agree with this quote? Why or why not?

Answer each question in a paragraph.

Our world and welcome to it...

"It was the best of times, it was the worst of times,
It was the age of wisdom, it was the age of foolishness,
It was the epoch of belief, it was the epoch of incredulity,
It was the season of Light, it was the season of Darkness,
It was the spring of hope, it was the winter of despair,
We had everything before us, we had nothing before us,
We were all going direct to Heaven, we were all going direct the other way —
In short, it was like the world we live in."   — Charles Dickens

Choose <u>three</u> of the above "opposite-type" statements and think about them in terms of our world <u>today</u>. In <u>six</u> paragraphs, using <u>SPECIFIC EXAMPLES</u>, show how the statement you have chosen holds true for <u>today's</u> world.

<u>Example</u>: If you pick "It was the age of wisdom, it was the age of foolishness," write a paragraph to discuss how <u>this</u> is an age of wisdom (in your opinion), and give <u>examples</u> to prove your point. In a second paragraph, show how this is <u>also</u> an age of foolishness. Again, give <u>examples</u>.

Listen...

1 Have you ever heard someone say, "Almost doesn't count." What do you think, does it or doesn't it? Why or why not? If "almost" counts, when does it count? If "almost" doesn't count, when doesn't it count? Give specific examples for both.

and

2 "Somewhere, a book once said, all the talk ever talked, all the songs ever sung, still lived and had vibrated way out in space and if you could travel far enough you could hear George Washington talking in his sleep or Caesar surprised at the knife in his back. So much for sounds. What about light then? All things once seen, they didn't just die, that couldn't be. It must be then that somewhere you might find all the colors and sights of the world in any one year." - Ray Bradbury

Can you put this quote into your own words? Do you agree? Why or why not? What sounds and sights are you glad are immortal? What sounds and sights would you rather have forgotten?

and

3 "Too many people don't know what they think until they hear someone else say it."

What does this quote mean? Do you agree with it? Why or why not? Does this ever happen to you? Why and when does this happen?

Visions...

An essay is a short, personal literary composition dealing with a single subject. Analyze the statements below and then follow this format for your essays.

Paragraph #1...Tell what the statement means. How does the meaning apply to you? Use specific examples.

Paragraph #2...Do you think the statement is true? In your opinion, is it an important statement? Answer both questions and tell why or why not.

You are to do this twice, once for each statement.

① "It's better to have loved and lost, than to have hated and won."

② "Some people see things that are, and ask why. Other people see things that are, and ask why not."

to teach or not to teach...

"The object of teaching a child is to enable him to get along without a teacher."

1. What do _you_ think this quotation means?
2. Do you agree with it? Why or why not?
3. What does education mean to _you_?
4. Does independence have anything to do with education? Why or why not?
5. What do _you_ think 'teaching' means?

---

if...

if coke is the real thing and lifesavers are a part of living, do you deserve a break today?

In several paragraphs answer this question yes or no, and write _WHY_. Before you write this assignment plug in your imagination. Then respond.

baseballs, hot dogs, apple pies & chevrolets...

A spaceman just landed in your town and knocks on your door...

Paragraph #1...What ten things that best represent American life would you show the spaceman, and WHY? Make them things you have in your house now.

Paragraph #2...What five foods would you serve the spaceman, and WHY? Try to choose foods that are representative of what Americans eat.

Paragraph #3...What two places would you take the spaceman to visit in your town, and WHY? Try to pick places that are in some way representative of America.

ANYWHERE U.S.A.

music and art...

CREATING...

For your assignment this week you will write on all _four_ quotations in either the music section _or_ the art section. You may _not_ do some from both categories. Choose one or the other. You will write _one_ paragraph for _each_ quotation. Answer the following questions for each quotation: What does the quote mean? Do you agree with it? Why or why not? Be as specific as you can, use "real-life" examples to prove your point... paintings or artists you know about, songs or musicians you know about. _Everyone_ will write about the quotation on creativity — what it means, do you agree or disagree with it, and why? Use examples from your _personal experience_.

MUSIC:

1- "Music is essentially useless, as life is." —GEORGE SANTAYANA

2- "Music is a way to give form to our inner feelings without attaching them to events or objects in the world." —GEORGE SANTAYANA

3- "Music was invented to confirm human lonliness." —LAWRENCE DURRELL

4- "A nation creates music—the composer only arranges it." —MIKHAIL GLINKA

music and art...

art:

1- "Every artist paints his own autobiography." - HAVELOCK ELLIS

2- "Art is meant to disturb." - GEORGES BRAQUE

3- "Art, like life, should be free, since both are experimental." - G. SANTAYANA

4- "Art does not <u>reproduce</u> the visible, rather, it <u>makes</u> visible." - PAUL KLEE

creativity:

1- "In creating, the only hard thing is to begin; a grass blade is no easier to make than an oak tree." - JAMES RUSSELL LOWELL

an eye for an eye... ?

LAW AND ORDER!

Answer these questions:

1. What is justice? Write your <u>own</u> definition. You may look up "justice" in the dictionary, but put the definition into <u>your</u> <u>own</u> <u>words</u>.

2. It is often said, "There is no justice in this world." If you agree with this statement, write <u>WHY</u> and give at least <u>two</u> specific examples to prove your point. If you disagree with this statement, write <u>WHY</u> and give at least <u>two</u> specific examples to prove your point.

3. Write one or two laws that <u>you</u> think should be written to protect kids. Write <u>why</u> you think there is a need for the law.

Changes...
"things do not change, we do." -THOREAU

Paragraph #1... Discuss how <u>things</u> do or do not change. Use specific examples.

Paragraph #2... Discuss how <u>people</u> do or do not change. Use specific examples.

Paragraph #3... Draw some conclusions - do you agree with this statement? Why or why not?

you be the judge...

A person commits a pre-meditated murder (it was planned.) The case goes to court. The jury finds the person guilty of 1st degree murder. The judge takes several hours to decide on sentencing and finally sentences the person to die in the electric chair. Two months later, the execution takes place.

Question: Should there be someone or something to decide whether or not the judge is guilty of murder and the jury is an accomplice to murder?

Explanation: The judge is "taking" the life of a person by sentencing the person to die - the jury finds the person guilty. So, can the judge and jury be held responsible for someone's murder?

Take one side of the question and argue your case. If you believe that someone should pass judgement on the judge and jury, write WHY you feel this way. Also, answer who should judge the judge and the jury. Also, how is sentencing someone to die the same as committing a murder.

If you believe that sentencing someone to die is not the same as committing a murder, write your reasons why.

BE CONVINCING - PRESENT A SOLID ARGUMENT!

don't assume anything...

These are some common assumptions in our culture. They <u>might</u> be true <u>or</u> they <u>might</u> be false. You must decide what is true or false for <u>you</u>. Be careful — you really need to think about each one and its <u>IMPLICATIONS</u>— what it suggests for people and their lives.

For each number decide whether <u>you</u> think it is <u>TRUE</u> or <u>FALSE</u>. Explain your answer. Back up your reasons with specific facts or examples. <u>How</u> do <u>you</u> know what you know and <u>what</u> makes <u>you</u> know if it is true or false? Also, <u>where</u> do you think the assumption comes from, or <u>how</u> do you think it got started?

1- People <u>need</u> cars.

2- People need to eat <u>three</u> meals a day.

3- People who go to college are smarter than people who don't.

4- Adults know more than children.

5- The most important thing a person can be is popular.

6- Men aren't good cooks.

7- Women take care of children better than men do.

8- Boys are better at sports than girls are.

9- Teachers know everything.

10- Pink is a girl's color.

don't assume anything...

11- The older a person gets the more responsible he or she gets.

12- The United States is a democratic country.

13- It's cheaper to eat at McDonalds than it is to eat at home.

14- Everything's better with Blue Bonnet on it.

15- Handicapped people are unhappy.

16- You can tell what a person is like by the way he or she looks.

17- At age eighteen you become an adult.

18- Grey hair is a sign of old age.

19- Coke is the real thing.

20- George Washington was our first president.

FACTOR FICTION?

II. creative writing...

IMAGINATION

to begin with...?

For your writing assignment this week you will write <u>two</u> separate paragraphs.

1 <u>My Block</u> (a description of the street you live on and how you feel about it.)

2 <u>If I Had One Million Dollars</u> (what would you do with it, <u>exactly</u>?)

---

two more...

For your writing assignment this week you will write <u>two</u> separate paragraphs.

1 <u>The Best Meal I Ever Had</u> (describe it, where did you eat it, who served it to you?)

2 <u>If I Could Be Any Age</u> (what age would you be and why?)

absence makes the heart grow fonder...

You have just been absent from school for three weeks...write an imaginary note with an imaginary excuse for your imaginary absence. Write it like a letter — make it at least a paragraph long.

---

paint...

If you could paint your town or city __any__ color, what color would you paint it and __why__? Answer this question in a paragraph or more. Imagine how...

Strange ...

Imagine that you found this ◖▬▶ in your <u>room</u>. Write about this thing in a paragraph or more. Include answers to these questions in your paragraphs:

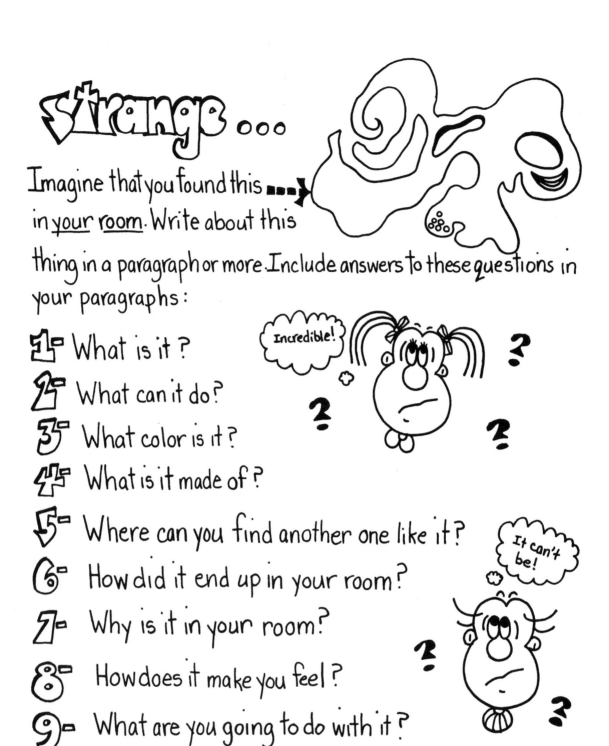

1. What is it?
2. What can it do?
3. What color is it?
4. What is it made of?
5. Where can you find another one like it?
6. How did it end up in your room?
7. Why is it in your room?
8. How does it make you feel?
9. What are you going to do with it?
10. How much do you think it is worth?

<u>Hint</u>: Let your imagination run wild. The out of the ordinary is fun to read.

directions...

Write <u>ten</u> sentences that begin with the words:

above me...

or

Write <u>ten</u> sentences that begin with the words:

below me...

or

Write <u>ten</u> sentences that begin with the words:

600 miles to the west of me...

or

Write <u>ten</u> sentences that begin with the words:

1000 light-years away from me, out in space...

Use your imagination to think of real <u>or</u> imaginary things... when you complete ten sentences, write one or two sentences summing up how the things you wrote about make you <u>feel</u>. The feeling checklist will help you.

Martians...

Imagine that you are a Martian scientist who has come to observe Earthlings at work and play. This is your first time on Earth and life on Mars is very different, so you have to make wild guesses about what is going on. What's more...you (as well as all other Martians) have NO HEARING. Choose three of the following things to explain to your Martian friends back home. Do this assignment in three paragraphs or more. Remember, you will have to describe these things as they appear to be - you don't know what they are, and you can't hear, either!

- your classroom.
- a supermarket.
- a baseball game.
- twelve midnight on New Year's Eve.
- McDonalds restaurant.
- a pajama party.
- a shopping center.
- a telephone.

- a trash compacter.
- someone shaving with an electric razor.
- a circus.
- a rock concert.
- a toothpick.
- a movie.
- someone yawning.
- a garden hose.

the door...

For your writing assignment this week you will write a story about <u>a door</u>.

Paragraph #1... Describe the door <u>in detail</u>. Your description checklist will help.

Paragraph #2... To what is the door attached? (House, bank, closet, castle, etc.) Explain and describe.

Paragraph #3... <u>What</u> is on the other side of the door? What is going on, <u>who or what</u> is there, <u>how</u> did it get there, <u>why</u> is it there?

Paragraph #4... What will happen when <u>you</u> open the door? Explain and describe.

Paragraph #5... Close your eyes and touch the door. Describe the feelings that touching the door gives you. The feeling checklist is helpful. Write a conclusion.

Astro Turf →

WELCOME

a captive audience

HELP! I'm trapped in a .....
- ..... supermarket
- ..... toy store
- ..... bakery
- ..... museum
- ..... a spaghetti factory
- ..... you choose one of your own

Choose <u>one</u> of the above places to be trapped in after hours. Now, write a story about your adventures after dark.

Paragraph #1... <u>Describe</u> where you are and how you happened to get locked in. <u>What</u> were you doing- <u>why</u> did it happen, <u>who</u> were you with?

Paragraph #2... Once you've discovered you're locked in and have some time to fool around, what will you do? Describe.

Paragraph #3... Plan your escape. How will you use what's in the store, factory, or museum to get out? What is your plan? Describe in detail.

Paragraph #4... How do you finally get out? Does your plan work? If not, why not, and what will you do? What happens when you get out? Describe. Write a conclusion to your story.

THE ADVENTURES of SUPER-KID

POW

faster than a speeding bullet...more powerful than a locomotive...

For your writing assignment this week, you will write a five paragraph story about an adventure of Super Kid.

Paragraph #1... Describe Super Kid. Use your description and feeling checklists. Be sure to include the kinds of powers he or she possesses.

Paragraph #2... Describe the <u>setting</u> of the story-exactly where and when does it take place.

Paragraph #3... In these two paragraphs you will develop the plot and
and   tell the actual story. Include at least <u>one problem</u>
Paragraph #4... Super Kid must face and solve.

Paragraph #5... This paragraph should be the conclusion, or ending to your story. Solve all problems, resolve all conflicts and tie up any loose ends. Try to write an interesting ending.

ZAP

The Wizard of Weird

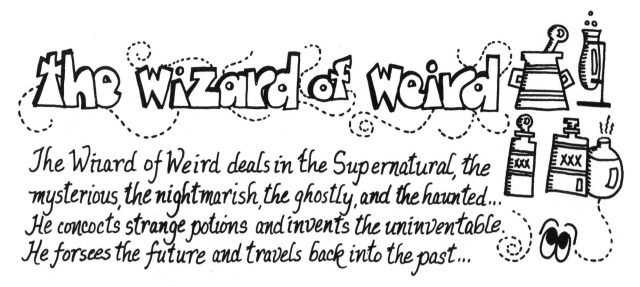

The Wizard of Weird deals in the Supernatural, the mysterious, the nightmarish, the ghostly, and the haunted... He concocts strange potions and invents the uninventable. He forsees the future and travels back into the past...

WRITE A STORY ABOUT THE WIZARD OF WEIRD...

Paragraph #1... Describe the Wizard. Use your description and feeling checklists. What kinds of things can he do? Use examples.

Paragraph #2... Describe the setting. Where and when does this story take place? Describe the Wizards' laboratory.

Paragraph #3... Use these two paragraphs to develop the plot of your story.
and   What happens? What does the Wizard do? Who does he do it

Paragraph #4... to, for, or with? How does he do it? Why does he do it?

Paragraph #5... Write a conclusion to your story.

108

the great _____ robbery
(fill in blank)

Robber

Choose <u>one</u> of the following to fill in the blank:
- a) peanut butter
- b) pickle
- c) pencil
- d) rubber band

You are going to write a story about the Great _____ Robbery.
(fill in)

Paragraph #1... Describe <u>where</u> and <u>when</u> the robbery takes place.

Paragraph #2... Describe the robbers. There are at least <u>three</u>. What are they like - looks, actions, personalities...

Paragraph #3... <u>Why</u> did the robbery take place? What did the robbers want to do with the loot?

Paragraph #4... <u>What</u> happened during the robbery? Describe the plan. <u>How</u> did it happen? <u>How</u> much did they take?

Paragraph #5... Did the robbers succeed? If so, how? What did they do with the loot, where did they go? If not, <u>why</u> not? What went wrong? Write a <u>conclusion</u> to your story.

Raw Steak Rides Again... ☆

The town is Dodge City...the date is January 5th, 1890. Raw Steak is a cowboy in the wild, wild west. His best friends are Wyatt Earp and The Lone Ranger. He has a pet cactus named Tex. Raw Steak is a deputy sheriff. He rides a trail-to-who-knows-where...

Write a story about Raw Steak using <u>one</u> of the following titles:

- Raw Steak Meets Godzilla.
- Raw Steak & the Silver Bullet.
- Raw Steak Discovers the Lost <u>(you fill in)</u>.
- Raw Steak Captures The Good, The Bad, & The Ugly.

This will be a <u>5</u> paragraph story. Begin with an interesting <u>first line</u>. Try to use dialogue that fits the old west. Remember, this is the time of stagecoaches, the Pony Express, cattle drives, etc. Use the outline below. You may write the paragraphs in any order you want. (In other words, you can start with the action, or the setting, or whatever...)

A. Description of Raw Steak & Tex. Use description checklist. Include appearance, personality, hobbies, etc.

B. Description of setting. Where and when does the story take place?

C. Plot, or actual story - <u>two</u> paragraphs. What happens? Who else is involved in the story? How does it happen? Why does it happen?

D. Conclusion. Try to write an interesting ending.

Oh, give me a home...

a detective I.M.Sharp Mystery

Presenting Detective I.M.Sharp in...The Case of the Hidden Diamond.

For your writing assignment this week, you will make up a mystery story. You may develop the case "any way you want, but make it revolve around a hidden diamond.

Paragraph #1... Describe the <u>setting</u> of your story - where does it take place? When does it happen? Write an exciting <u>first line</u>. ← diamond

Paragraph #2... Describe <u>Detective</u> <u>I.M.</u> <u>Sharp</u>. Use your description and feeling checklists. How long has he been a detective? What does the "I.M." stand for? For whom does he work? How did he get involved in this case? Who hired him? ← clue GULP ← fear ! ← suspense

Paragraph #3... Discuss the <u>diamond</u>. How many carats; how large; what does it look like; to whom does it belong; does it have a legend or story behind it, like the Hope Diamond; what is its history; does it have a curse that goes along with it; what is it worth? HELP! ← drama

Paragraph #4... These 2 paragraphs will tell your story. Be sure to include:
and <u>who</u> hid the diamond, <u>why</u> was it hidden, <u>where</u> was it hidden,
Paragraph #5... <u>how</u> was it hidden, <u>when</u> was it hidden? ? ← mystery

Paragraph #6... <u>Conclusion</u> to your story. Try to build up suspense. How does I.M.Sharp recover the diamond (or does he?) Your ending should be as exciting and interesting as your first line. ← mysterious footprints

Smog City, USA

Write a story about a city that pollutes itself to extinction (ALMOST!)

Paragraph #1... Where and when does this story take place? Describe the city in detail. This can be a real city or an imaginary city.

Paragraph #2... Describe <u>three</u> people who live in this city - who are they; what do they do; how do they act? Use your description checklist.

Paragraph #3... <u>How</u> does the pollution overtake the city? <u>What</u> happens; <u>how</u> long does it take; <u>why</u> does it happen?

Paragraph #4... <u>Who</u> saves the city? <u>How</u> is it saved? <u>Why</u> is it saved?

Paragraph #5... <u>What</u> does the city do to make sure that this problem <u>won't</u> happen again? What is the long range plan? Write a conclusion to your story.

smog↘

↙Pollution

foward into the past...

Time Flies Backwards!

Imagine that you have gone into a time machine that transports you back to a <u>primitive</u> world in which creatures that are <u>now</u> <u>small</u>, are very big and powerful, and creatures that are <u>now large</u>, are very small and weak. Also imagine that you are by yourself and that you have not found any signs of human civilization.

Write a five-paragraph story about what you see (describe) and what you have to do to survive. Be sure to include: an interesting opening line; how big or small things are; what they look like; what experiences you have; how you solve problems as they occur; and how you feel while you are there. You can write the entire story about <u>one</u> creature, or about several different ones.

BUZZ ZZZ...

GULP!

10 feet

KEEP OUT!

MAIL

WELCOME

it all happened when...

You are going to write a story about:

1 How people learned the meaning of friendship

or

2 How people learned the meaning of loneliness

This assignment will be at least five paragraphs long. This is to be a <u>fable</u> and should be imaginary, although you can base your story on facts. Before you begin, decide what friendship or lonliness means to <u>you</u>.

Be sure to include: setting (where and when), description of any characters in your story, what happens, how it happens, and why it happens. Write an interesting first line.

rock around the clock...

Imagine yourself in the 1950's. Young people were interested in motorcycles, gangs, hot rods, sock hops, and beach parties. The stars of the day were James Dean, Elvis Presley, Chubby Checker, and the Marines. Girls wore full skirts, straight skirts, and bobby socks, and were always trying to snag the most popular boys in school to go on a date to the malt shop or a drive-in movie. Guys walked around in their letter sweaters or black leather jackets, loafers, peggers, or pointy shoes, trying to make time with a good-looking "chick."

Imagine yourself in the 1950's. You may be anyone you wish. Write a story about one experience you had in the 1950's. Your story should be approximately six paragraphs long. Have at least three characters in your story. Describe and develop their personalities and appearances. Describe your setting. Include: <u>what</u> happened, <u>how</u> it happened, <u>why</u> it happened, <u>when</u> it happened, <u>where</u> it happened, and <u>who</u> it happened to.

Here are some words that were used in the 1950's. To create the proper atmosphere, use at least <u>fifteen</u> of them in your story. Ask your parents and "older" friends for ideas too. Do some research to find out what times were really like then...

rock around the clock...

sheen = car
crazy = wild
bohemian = hippie
beatnik = hippie
keen = terrific
malted = milkshake
fuzz = police
fink = to tell on someone
rat = to tell on someone
boss = cool
platter = record
hip = cool
hot rod = souped up car
ducktail = slicked back hair

drag = car race
hang-a-Louie = take a left
hang-a-Ralph = take a right
sock hop = a prom-type dance
pad = house
kooky = out of the ordinary
bopping = type of dance
chick = girl
peggers = tapered pants
down = feeling low
D.J. = disc jockey
New Yorker = a type of dance
Lindy = a type of dance
suedes = shoes

daddy'o/ hey, man...

Like crazy!

See you in September 🔮

For your writing assignment this week, you are going to write a four paragraph story about what you want to be doing on the afternoon of September 22, 1999. (Figure out how old you will be in 1999.)

Paragraph #1... <u>WHERE</u> will you be?

Paragraph #2... <u>WHAT</u> will you be doing?

Paragraph #3... <u>WHO</u> will you be with that afternoon? Why will they be there? If you will be alone, why will you be alone? How will you feel?

Paragraph #4... <u>WHY</u> do you want to be doing this? What will it accomplish in your life? Will you have to prepare for doing this? How?

Time Flies...

Once upon a time...

Write a story about:

1ᵉ How People Learned to Laugh... <u>or</u>

2ᵉ How People Learned to Care for Other People... <u>or</u>

3ᵉ How People Learned to Cry.

Once upon a time...

This assignment will be done in five paragraphs. Be as descriptive as you can. This is to be a <u>fable</u> and should be "made-up," although you can base your story on facts. Be sure to include: <u>WHERE</u> it happened, <u>WHEN</u> it happened, <u>WHO</u> was involved, <u>WHAT</u> happened, <u>WHY</u> it happened, and <u>HOW</u> it happened.

<u>Hint</u>: Before you begin, try to remember the first time you started caring for others, thought something was really funny, or cried...

how it came to be...

For your writing assignment this week, you will write a myth or legend about how <u>one</u> of the following came to be:

    1- How Mountains Came To Be

    2- How the Hamburger Came To Be

    3- How Music Came To Be

    4- How Football Came To Be

    5- How Washing Machines Came To Be

    6- How the Alphabet Came To Be

This is to be a six paragraph story. Be sure to include:

<u>WHAT</u> happened.	<u>WHO</u> was involved.
<u>WHERE</u> it happened.	<u>HOW</u> it happened.
<u>WHEN</u> it happened.	<u>WHY</u> it happened.

Describe in detail. Explain everything. Have a great opening sentence. Write an interesting ending.

You may use this outline in any order:

- Introduction and Setting (Where and When)

- Who was involved

- What happened, how did it happen, why did it happen? (approximately three paragraphs.)

- Conclusion (ending.)

III. UNITS...

INTRODUCTION

Several times during the course of the school year, we found it both necessary and worthwhile to depart from the Basal-Reading System to implement week-long units that gave the students the opportunity to put their "reading knowledge" to use as well as to increase their awareness of the world through diverse contemporary pieces. These units came to be because we both believed that reading should not be taught as a sacred and unapproachable skill exclusive of life, and more importantly, we wanted our reading material to reflect and investigate human values that would support critical thinking, decision-making, and the idea of survival. In the absence of any "packaged system" that met our goals, we turned to creating our own materials.

The units included here fall into two basic categories: reading comprehension strategies and perceptual interpretations, and investigations of various literary forms. One essential idea behind these units was to make these reading and writing exercises enjoyable and interesting for the student. In keeping with this objective, we structured the units in the following manner. Each unit covered one week and was substituted in place of the regular reading program, for an hour and a half each day. Writing and Spelling assignments were handed out and explained first thing on Monday. The Spelling assignment was done individually and was handed in when completed by the student, to be checked by a teacher and returned promptly. Spelling words were reviewed in groups, some time during the Thursday period, with a Spelling test given at the beginning of the Friday period. (Spelling tests corresponded to the spelling assignment. We asked one question for each word and tested for synonyms, usage in a sentence, definition, part of speech, and matching the definition with the word, in addition to spelling the word.) Students had until Thursday to complete their writing assignments. We required each student to write a rough draft as well as a final copy (in ink with a minimum of mistakes). Rough drafts were due by Thursday, at the beginning of the reading period. Before handing them in to a teacher, each student was responsible for proof-reading his or her paper. Rough drafts were then checked for content and structural mistakes. Correcting the rough draft took the form of "conferences" with each student. Final copies were due at the end of the day on Friday. (As the year went on, the students learned how to budget their time according to their capabilities and comfort level. Some students handed in their rough drafts on Tuesday, while others waited until Thursday. However, for each unit, we made certain that most required work could be completed in the allotted classroom time).

The actual reading material was handed out each day; usually one assignment per day. We re-distributed the students into "new" reading groups (mixing high and low ability students) and aimed for groups which we felt would be compatible for stimulating discussions. Students read individual copies of the song or poem or story, and were encouraged to interpret and answer the questions with a minimum of teacher explanation. Students requiring explanations were given individual help. We stressed the need for *quality* in their answers, and emphasized that they would be responsible for defending their answers. (Our philosophy was that there were few, if any, "right" or "wrong" answers and that the quality of their work depended on how well they could reason and defend what they had to say.) When completing the initial assignment for the day, the students were given the rest of the time to work on their spelling and writing assignments. (During this time, the teachers corrected rough drafts and spelling and generally helped students with any problems relating to the assignments, and made sure everyone was progressing toward completion.) Approximately thirty minutes before the end of each reading period, everyone stopped what they were doing and broke up into their "discussion groups". During this time the reading assignment and questions for the day were reviewed. This was a time for explanation and interpretation, going over questions, asking new ones, sharing feelings and in general, "going wherever the conversation led." More often than not, the students became quite involved in exploring their personalities, their lives, and the world around them.

spell and write...

Spelling Stories...

DICTIONARY

For your writing assignment this week, you will write a story using __ALL__ of your spelling words in it. Do your spelling words first. Get the definition, the part of speech, and a synonym for each word. Then, look at all your definitions and think of a story (any story) that would involve all the words. Let your imagination run wild. The story will be at least five paragraphs long.

the words:

fragile	annex	unkempt
rotund	fable	sinister
trivial	chaos	antique
murmur	lucrative	extravagant
meager	magenta	taut

<u>Teacher</u>: Change the words according to the spelling ability of the students.

124

spelling stories...

Words have a special power. With them you are able to create <u>images</u>. For the words below, look up the definition, part of speech, and find a synonym for each word. Then, write about what the word <u>really</u> means. Create an image of that word. Write a paragraph for <u>each</u> word. Make each paragraph <u>fit</u> the word.

1- forlorn

2- interdependence

3- heritage

4- melancholy

5- apparition

writing the news...

Each student receives one fairly current <u>Time</u> or <u>Newsweek</u> magazine and reads it from cover-to-cover. The magazines can be different for each student. During the allotted time period for this activity, each pupil is responsible for reading his or her magazine, answering the corresponding questions ("I Have a Question,") completing the writing assignment ("What's New?,") and the spelling assignment.

what's new?

...Today in the news...

"Nowadays truth is the greatest news..." —THOMAS FULLER, M.D

" How many beautiful trees gave their lives so that today's scandel
   should, without delay, reach a million readers!..." — EDWIN WAY TEALE

" A good newspaper, I suppose, is a Nation talking to itself..." —ARTHUR MILLER

" People everywhere confuse what they read in newspapers with news..."—A.J. LIEBLING

" The window to the world can be covered by a newspaper..." —STANISLAW LEC.

" The evil that Men do lives on the front pages of greedy newspapers, but the
   good they do is often buried with little concern inside..."—BROOKS ATKINSON

" News is popular, but it is popular mainly as fiction. Life is one world, and
   life seen in the news is another..." —G·K·CHESTERTON

Choose any <u>three</u> quotations. For each quote you will write <u>two</u> paragraphs. Use
examples to help you express your thoughts and feelings.

Paragraph #1... Explain the quotation. Do you agree with it? Why or why not?
                What is the point (or purpose) of this quote?

Paragraph #2... How does this quote apply or relate to what you've been
                reading this week?

i have a question ...

You will be responsible for answering all of these questions...use your magazine to find the answers.

1- In your opinion, what is the most newsworthy (valuable) story in your magazine? Why is it so important? What is it about?

2- What point does the editorial in your magazine make? What is it about? How well does the editor prove his or her point?

3- What type of letters to the editor are in your magazine? Are they mostly favorable or unfavorable? Can you tell what type of people seem to read these magazines from the letters?

4- What is the cover story about? Summarize it. How well is the story covered? Does it leave you asking any questions? If so, what?

5- What kinds of ads are found in your magazine? Do they fall into certain groups? Why do you suppose these types of ads are in the magazine?

6- It has been said, "One picture is worth a thousand words." What picture in your magazine applies to this statement? In other words, which picture is most expressive? Why? What is the story that goes along with the picture? Cut the picture out and attach it to your answers.

7- Do the stories in the Education Section apply to your education? Why or why not?

8- Of all the book or movie reviews in your magazine, which one is the most convincing? Why? If none were, why not?

i have a question...

9· Find one example of an <u>international</u> news story. What is it about? Find an example of a <u>national</u> news story. What is it about? What is the difference between an international and national news story?

10· In your opinion, what person in the news was most interesting to read about? Why? What did s/he do?

11· Rewrite any one news story (of your choice) as a <u>fictional</u> (imaginary) story.

12· What is the style or mood of a news story? How is a news story written to make it different from a fictional story?

13· Is there any humor in the news? Find an example of a humorous news story and tell what it is about and why you think it is funny.

14· Copy one headline you found in your magazine. Write about how it <u>fits</u> the story. Why or why not is this a good title for the story?

15· Choose one sports story and summarize it.

16· Find the Law Section. Do any of the stories concern <u>human rights</u>? If so, how? If not, what are the stories about?

Write the definition, part of speech, and a synonym. Use <u>each</u> word in a fifteen line poem (it doesn't have to rhyme) about the news. You may change the order of the words.

1. celebrity
2. economy
3. update
4. columnist
5. objectivity

6. analysis
7. policy
8. opinion
9. forum
10. editorial

11. correspondent
12. international
13. recession
14. newsworthy
15. transition

✸ Try to find the meaning that applies to the <u>NEWS</u>.

holidays...

These activities offer the student an opportunity to involve language arts with the holiday seasons. The student will be asked to write stories, create cards, use spelling words that have holiday connotations, and to give a personal interpretation to a holiday.

HAPPY...

which witch ?

WRITE ONE PARAGRAPH AND MAKE IT SCARY!

The <u>words</u> you choose will help create a mood of absolute terror. Use Halloween-type adjectives. Be careful, this is harder than it sounds. You only have <u>one</u> paragraph in which to frighten your reader. Try to create your mood by using descriptive words rather than by relying on your subject matter.

This is the season of the witch

Choose **one** of the following titles and write a scary story!

1~ The Vampire Dies at Midnight
2~ The Icy Fingers of Doom
3~ The Ghost of Count Dracula

This will be a five paragraph story. Be descriptive. Be sure to include: setting (where and when), descriptions of all the characters, an interesting opening line, and a conclusion. Answer these questions: <u>WHAT</u> happens, <u>WHY</u> does it happen, <u>WHO</u> does it happen to, and <u>HOW</u> does it happen?

Spelling horrors

1. frighten	6. appalling	11. eerie	16. corpse	21. alarming
2. panic	7. dreadful	12. gruesome	17. phantom	22. suspicious
3. haunted	8. tremble	13. macabre	18. sorcery	23. shadow
4. terror	9. hideous	14. sinister	19. doom	24. jittery
5. petrify	10. ghoulish	15. ominous	20. mysterious	25. apparition

Choose fifteen of these words to use in your creative writing story. <u>Underline</u> the words you use in your story.

gratitude... Thanksgiving is the time of year when people are especially aware of things for which they are thankful...

Write <u>two</u> thank you notes to <u>two</u> different people and thank them for something they have done for you during this past year.

1- You may thank anyone you know - a relative, friend, acquaintance, etc.

2- Write these as you would a "thank you note." Use two pieces of paper.

3- Be sure to include an explanation of <u>what</u> it was that this person did for you - <u>where</u> and <u>when</u> they have done it for you, <u>why</u> you are thankful for what this person has done (why does it mean something to you) and <u>how</u> you feel about it.

4- Make each note one paragraph in length.

FORM

DATE

DEAR _____ ,

YOUR LETTER

_____ YOUR NAME

THANK YOU

<u>Example:</u>

November 24, 1975

To All of You,

Somehow, in the course of a school day, many things that should get said, never do. We'd like to take this opportunity to say thank you to all of you for something we consider important. We think that one of the nicest things about teaching is the chance it presents for us to learn from you. Through you, and because of you, we are constantly learning things about ourselves as people, as adults, and teachers. Without all of you, this wouldn't be possible. So you are important to us for this reason, and others. Thank you for being you...

Mrs. Maid and Mr. Wallace

Gobble... Thanks ooo

Turkey

For your writing assignment this week, choose #1 or #2.

1 Write a Thanksgiving story from a turkey's point of view. Be sure to include the sights, sounds, smells, and tastes of the holiday. Describe things. Answer these questions: WHERE does the story take place, WHEN does it take place, WHAT happens, HOW does it happen, and WHY does it happen. This is to be a six paragraph story.

or

2 Write a Thanksgiving story that takes place in the year 2001 (in a futuristic society.) Be sure to include the sights, sounds, smells, and tastes of the holiday. What will Thanksgiving be like in the future...will everyone go out to eat at Kentucky Fried Turkey, will Plymouth Rock have fallen into the ocean, will people be taking rocket trips to their relative's houses? Describe things. Answer these questions: WHO is the story about, WHERE does the story take place, WHAT happens, WHY does it happen, and WHAT WILL PEOPLE IN THE YEAR 2001 BE THANKFUL ABOUT? This is to be a six paragraph story.

words for which to be thankful...

1. aroma
2. celebration
3. savory
4. gratitude
5. succulent
6. ritual
7. appetite
8. devour

9. edible
10. gastronomy
11. poultry
12. entrée
13. nourishment
14. gorge
15. pilgrimage
16. cornucopia

PILGRIM ←

✱ Pick the definition that best applies to Thanksgiving.
Use at least <u>six</u> of the words in your creative writing story and <u>underline</u> them in your story.

BOAT ↓

MAYFLOWER

PLYMOUTH ROCK ↓

1620

happy holiday

This is the season for giving. Many people give and receive gifts. You will write a short, three paragraph story about a gift you have received that you <u>didn't</u> want. This can be imaginary if this has never happened to you, but try to use a real-life example.

Paragraph #1... What is the gift. Describe it in detail. You can also describe the outside of the package — size, wrapping, etc.

Paragraph #2... Write about your feelings <u>before</u> you opened the package and how you felt <u>after</u> you saw the gift. Use the feeling checklist for help.

Paragraph #3... Okay, so you don't like the gift. Think of a person that could <u>really</u> use (or might want) this gift. Write <u>who</u> you would give this gift to and <u>why</u>. (It isn't enough to say a needy person, what kind of needy person — who, <u>specifically</u>?)

Now, answer this question in a few sentences:

Do <u>you</u> agree with this statement —

    It's not the gift that counts, it's the thought behind it.

Write yes or no, and answer <u>WHY</u>.

when you care enough to ?👀 send the very best...?👀

Since this is the season when people's thoughts turn to peace and goodwill toward others, your writing assignment this week will be to design and compose a <u>card</u> expressing <u>your</u> feelings or beliefs about "<u>PEACE</u>." This is <u>not</u> to be a Christmas or Hanukah card.

You will be responsible for creating a coherent and meaningful design for the front of your card. This will be a design of your own choosing (drawing, collage, pen and ink, etc.) Be creative. Use your imagination. You may combine art techniques and use assorted mediums (charcoal, pastels, ink, scraps of material, wood, etc.) You may need to bring in some materials from home for this project. You will be responsible for collecting the things you need. <u>THE DESIGN IS TO BE RELATED TO YOUR MESSAGE</u>.

For the inside of the card, write a message conveying one or several of your ideas about "Peace on Earth." (Note that there is more than one kind of peace — there is "<u>inner</u> peace" as well as "<u>world</u> peace." Your message can take the form of <u>two</u> paragraphs, a poem, or prose. Carefully consider what you write. Trite descriptions or clichés (things that everybody says) may be worn out messages. This message will be <u>your</u> statement (feelings) you would like to share about peace.

Once your message is written, consider <u>placement</u> (layout) of the words on the paper. <u>Where</u> and <u>how</u> you place your words can be as important as the message itself.

The <u>inside</u> of your card can be as artistic as the <u>outside</u>... which means beautiful printing or script.

Your rough draft can be sketched on the outside of your card, <u>plus</u> the <u>EXACT</u> message you plan to put on the inside.

138

New Year's Resolutions...

A resolution is a promise that says you will do something at a later date. People usually have a hard time keeping their resolutions. Let's not worry about the future. What bothers you about you, NOW? (Even if you can't do anything about it this year.) In other words, what would you like to change about the way you act? Answer this question in one paragraph or more.

Spelling for the holidays

snow

1. tranquillity
2. harmony
3. calm
4. yuletide
5. frigid

6. blizzard
7. icicle
8. glacier
9. snowbound
10. goodwill

11. prosperity
12. avalanche
13. boughs (of holly)
14. tinsel
15. brotherhood

Look up the definition, part of speech, and write a synonym for each word. Now, write a fifteen line poem (it doesn't have to rhyme) using one of the spelling words in each line. You may change the order of the words if you want.

moods...

Each child will be responsible for completing the writing and spelling assignments as well as reading "Mood Paragraphs," "Moods in Poetry," a short story, and answering related questions.

We used the short story "After Twenty Years" by O. Henry, but any short story creating a specific mood will work.

miscellaneous moods...

Mood is a state of mind or feeling. Read these paragraphs and pay particular attention to the <u>moods</u> they try to develop. When you finish reading, go back over the paragraphs and <u>underline</u> those words which you think help create the mood of the paragraph. Also, check (✓) those paragraphs which you think most successfully create a certain mood or tone. Be prepared to defend your choices. Consider <u>how</u> the mood was created.

The sidewalks were haunted by dust ghosts all night as the furnace wind summoned them up, swung them about, and gentled them down in a warm spice on the lawns. Trees, shaken by the footsteps of late-night strollers, sifted avalanches of dust. From midnight on, it seemed a volcano beyond the town was showering red-hot ashes everywhere, crusting slumberless night watchmen and irritable dogs. Each house was a yellow attic smoldering with spontaneous combusion at three in the morning.

Dawn, then, was a time where things changed element for element. Air ran like hot spring waters nowhere, with no sound. The lake was a quantity of steam very still and deep over valleys of fish and sand held baking under its serene vapors. Tar was poured licorice in the streets, red bricks were brass and gold, roof tops were paved with bronze. The high-tension wires were lightening held forever, blazing, a threat above the unslept houses.

The cicadas sang louder and yet louder.

The sun did not rise, it overflowed.

Ray Bradbury, **Dandelion Wine**

She wore a dark striped dress reaching down to her shoe tops, and an equally long apron of bleached sugar sacks, with a full pocket: all neat and tidy, but every time she took a step she might have fallen over her shoelaces, which dragged from her unlaced shoes. She looked straight ahead. Her eyes were blue with age. Her skin had a pattern all its own of numberless branching wrinkles, and as though a whole little tree stood in the middle of her forehead, but a golden color ran underneath, and the two knobs of her cheeks were illumined by a yellow burning under the dark. Under the red rag her hair came down on her neck in the frailest of ringlets, still black, and with an odor like copper.

Eudora Welty, "A Worn Path"

Mother, in her pink apron with her hair in curlers, was leaning over the oven of the gas stove basting the turkey. Glenn was standing beside her with his mouth watering as he watched the little splashes of juice sizzle as they trickled off the kitchen spoon onto the brown tight skin of the turkey.

John Dos Passos, "Red, White, and
Blue Thanksgiving"

miscellaneous moods...

The garden grew as by a miracle, and the blackberry winter passed with the early April winds, doing no harm. Beans broke their waxen leaves out of hoe-turned furrows, bearing the husk of the seeds with them. Sweet corn unfurled tight young blades from weed mold, timid to night chill, growing slowly and darkly. Crows hung on blue air, surveying the patch, but the garden was too near the house. Our shouts and swift running through the tended ground kept them frightened and filled with wonder.

James Still, "Mole-Bane"

She hurried into a new spring evening dress of the frailest fairy blue. In the excitement of seeing herself in it, it seemed as if she had shed the old skin of winter and emerged a shining chrysalis with no stain; and going downstairs her feet fell softly just off the beat of the music from below. It was a tune from a play she had seen a week ago in New York, a tune with a future—ready for gayeties as yet unthought of, lovers not yet met. Dancing off, she was certain that life had innumerable beginnings. She had hardly gone ten steps when she was cut in upon by Donald Knowleton. She soared skyward on a rocket of surprise and delight.

F. Scott Fitzgerald, "A Woman with a Past"

The barn was blank as a blind face. The lantern was flickering, and in that witching light the stalls and the heap of sleighs, plows, old harness, at the back wall of the barn were immense and terrifying. The barn was larger than his whole house in Brooklyn, and ten times as large it seemed in the dimness. He could not see clear to the back wall, and he imagined abominable monsters lurking there. He dashed at the ladder up to the haymow, the lantern handle in his teeth and his imitation-leather satchel in one hand.

Sinclair Lewis, "Land"

In the assembling plant everyone works "on the belt." This is a big steel conveyor, a kind of moving sidewalk, waist-high. It is a great river running down through the plant. Various tributary streams come into the main stream, the main belt. They bring tires, they bring headlights, horns, bumpers for cars. They flow into the main stream. The main stream has its source at the freight cars, where the parts are unloaded, and it flows out to the other end of the factory and into other freight cars. The finished automobiles go into the freight cars at the delivery end of the belt. The assembly plant is a place of peculiar tension. You feel it when you go in. It never lets up. Men here work always on tension. There is no let-up to the tension. If you can't stand it, get out.

Sherwood Anderson, "Lift Up Thine Eyes"

More Moods... OPPOSITE? mood?

Write one word that you feel expresses the mood for each paragraph.
Now, re-write any two of the three paragraphs and write each one so that
the paragraph will express the opposite mood.

The pass was high and wide and he jumped for it, feeling it slap flatly against his hands, as he shook his hips to throw off the halfback who was diving at him. The center floated by, his hands desperately brushing Darling's knee as Darling picked his feet up high and delicately ran over a blocker and an opposing linesman in a jumble on the ground near the scrimmage line. He had ten yards in the clear and picked up speed, breathing easily, feeling his thigh pad rising and falling against his legs, listening to the sound of cleats behind him, pulling away from them, watching the other backs heading him off toward the sideline, the whole picture, the men closing in on him, the blockers fighting for position, the ground he had to cross, all suddenly clear in his head, for the first time in his life not a meaningless confusion of men, sounds, speed. He smiled a little to himself as he ran, holding the ball lightly in front of him with his two hands, his knees pumping high, his hips twisting in the almost girlish run of a back in a broken field. The first halfback came at him and he fed him his leg, them swung at the last moment, took the shock of the man's shoulder without breaking stride, ran right through him, his cleats biting securely into the turf. There was only the safety man now, coming warily at him, his arms crooked, hands spread. Darling tucked the ball in, spurted at him, driving hard, hurling himself along, all two hundred pounds bunched into controlled attack. He was sure he was going to get past the safety man. Without thought, his arms and legs working beautifully together, he headed right for the safety man, stiff-armed him, feeling blood spurt instantaneously from the man's nose onto his hand, seeing his face go awry, head turned, mouth pulled to one side. He pivoted away, keeping the arm locked, dropping the safety man as he ran easily toward the goal line, with the drumming of cleats diminishing behind him.
Irwin Shaw, "The Eighty-Yard Run"

It was a magnificent July day, one of those days which come only when the weather has been fair for a long time. From the very earliest dawn the sky is clear; the morning glow does not flame like a conflagration: it pours itself forth in a gentle flush. The sun, not fiery, not red-hot, as in the season of sultry drought, not of a dull crimson, as before a tempest, but bright, and agreeably radiant, glides up peacefully under a long, narrow cloudlet, beams freshly, and plunges into its lilac mist. The thin upper edges of the outstretched cloudlet begins to flash like darting serpents; their gleam resembles the gleam of hammered silver . . .
Ivan Turgenev, "Byezhin Meadow"

more moods...

He stood for a moment looking about. Behind him the rain whirled at the door. Ahead of him, upon a low table, stood a silver pot of hot chocolate, steaming, and a cup, full, with a marshmallow in it. And beside that, on another tray, stood thick sandwiches of rich chicken meat and fresh-cut tomatoes and green onions. And on a rod just before his eyes was a great thick green Turkish towel, and a bin in which to throw wet clothes, and, to his right, a small cubicle in which heat rays might dry you instantly. And upon a chair, a fresh change of uniform, waiting for anyone—himself, or any lost one—to make use of it. And farther over, coffee in steaming copper urns, and a phonograph from which music was playing quietly, and books bound in red and brown leather. And near the books a cot, a soft deep cot upon which one might lie, exposed and bare, to drink in the rays of the one great bright thing which dominated the long room . . . He was looking at the sun.

Ray Bradbury, **The Illustrated Man**

The rain continued. It was a hard rain, a perpetual rain, a sweating and steaming rain; it was a drizzle, a downpour; a fountain, a whipping at the eyes, an undertow at the ankles; it was a rain to drown all rains and the memory of rains. It came by the pound and the ton, it hacked at the jungle and cut the trees like scissors and shaved the grass and tunneled the soil and molted the bushes. It shrank men's hands into the hands of wrinkled apes; it rained a solid glassy rain, and it never stopped . . . The lieutenant looked up. He had a face that once had been brown and now the rain has washed it pale, and the rain had washed the color from his eyes and they were white, as were his teeth, and as was his hair. He was all white. Even his uniform was beginning to turn white, and perhaps a little green with fungus.

Ray Bradbury, **The Illustrated Man**

moods in poetry...

What moods do you find in these poems? Write <u>one</u> or <u>two</u> words that express the mood of <u>each</u> poem. How does each poet create the mood in his or her poem? What differences are there in creating moods for poetry rather than prose?

Lucy in the Sky with Diamonds
John Lennon and Paul McCartney

Picture yourself in a boat on a river,
With tangerine trees and marmalade skies
Somebody calls you, you answer quite slowly,
A girl with kaleidoscope eyes.
Cellophane flowers of yellow and green,
Towering over your head.
Look for the girl with the sun in her eyes,
And she's gone.
Lucy in the sky with diamonds.

Follow her down to a bridge by a fountain
Where rocking horse people eat marshmallow pies,
Everyone smiles as you drift past the flowers,
That grow so incredibly high.
Newspaper taxis appear on the shore,
Waiting to take you away.
Climb in the back with your head in the clouds.
And you're gone.
Lucy in the sky with diamonds.

Picture yourself on a train in a station,
With plasticine porters with looking glass ties,
Suddenly someone is there at the turnstile,
The girl with kaleidoscope eyes.

moods in poetry...

The Word "Plum"
Helen Chasin

The word "plum" is delicious

pout and push, luxury of
self-love, and savoring murmur

full in the mouth and falling
like fruit

taut skin
pierced, bitten, provoked into
juice, and tart flesh

question
and reply, lip and tongue
of pleasure.

Ozymandias
Percy Bysshe Shelley

I met a traveler from an antique land
Who said: Two vast and trunkless legs of stone
Stand in the desert . . . Near them, on the sand,
Half sunk, a shattered visage lies, whose frown,
And wrinkled lip, and sneer of cold command,
Tell that its sculptor well those passions read
Which yet survive, stamped on these lifeless things,
The hand that mocked them, and the heart that fed:
And on the pedestal these words appear:
"My name is Ozymandias, King of Kings:
Look on my works, ye mighty, and despair!"
Nothing beside remains. Round the decay
Of that colossal wreck, boundless and bare
The lone and level sands stretch far away.

146

moods in poetry...

Foul Shot
Edwin A. Hoey

With two 60's stuck on the scoreboard
And two seconds hanging on the clock,
The solemn boy in the center of eyes,
Squeezed by silence,
Seeks out the line with his feet,
Soothes his hands along his uniform,
Gently drums the ball against the floor,
Then measures the waiting net,
Raises the ball on his right hand,
Balances it with his left,
Calms it with fingertips,
Breathes,
Crouches,
Waits,
And then through a stretching of stillness,
Nudges it upward.

The ball
Slides up and out,
Lands,
Leans,
Wobbles,
Wavers,
Hesitates,
Exasperates,
Plays it coy
Until every face begs with unsounding screams—
And then
                                        And then
                                        And then,
Right before ROAR-UP,
Dives down and through.

147

moods in poetry...

Resume
Dorothy Parker

Razors pain you;
Rivers are damp;
Acids stain you;
And drugs cause cramp.
Guns aren't lawful;
Nooses give;
Gas smells awful;
You might as well live.

Gone Forever
Barris Mills

Halfway through shaving, it came—
the word for a poem.
I should have scribbled it on the mirror with a soapy finger,
or shouted it to my wife in the kitchen,
or muttered it to myself till it ran
in my head like a tune.

But now it's gone with whiskers
down the drain. Gone forever,
like the girls I never kissed,
and the places I never visited—
the lost lives I never lived.

148

Spelling

ooo Write the definition and part of speech. Then write a twenty line poem using each of the spelling words. You may change the order of the words. The poem does <u>not</u> have to rhyme.

1. morose
2. convoluted
3. dreary
4. whimsical
5. colossal
6. lethargic
7. tremulous
8. jaunty
9. effervescent
10. treacherous
11. mangy
12. permeate
13. gaudy
14. gelid
15. sultry
16. phantasmagoria
17. onomatopoeia
18. musty
19. mellow
20. illimitable

<u>Teacher</u>: Vary these words to your students' ability.

Creating your own moods ooo

Examine the list below:

1. gloominess
2. loneliness
3. terror
4. depression
5. frustration
6. coldness
7. wealth
8. poverty
9. darkness
10. warmth
11. humorous
12. defeat
13. agony
14. joy
15. chaos
16. crowded
17. irony
18. uneasiness
19. despair
20. bitterness
21. helplessness
22. happiness
23. violence
24. sinister
25. mysterious
26. astonishment
27. dullness
28. laziness

You will choose <u>ten</u> words from this list and you will write ten separate paragraphs expressing the "mood" of the word. The paragraphs are to be totally <u>unrelated</u>. Each paragraph will have to fit the mood of the word. This can be done in <u>two</u> ways: by descriptive words and situations, and the way in which your words are placed on the paper. Use the descriptive checklists.

Science Fiction...

Each child will choose his or her own <u>SCIENCE FICTION</u> book. After reading the book, each child will write a two paragraph summary of the book as follows: Paragraph #1... Explain the plot.

Paragraph #2... What is the <u>science fiction</u> in your book?

The child will also be responsible for reading the short story, "EPICAC" by Kurt Vonnegut and answering the related questions, completing the writing assignment and the spelling assignment, and reading the two poems and answering the related questions. The student will also be responsible for taking part in group discussions on all of the above assignments.

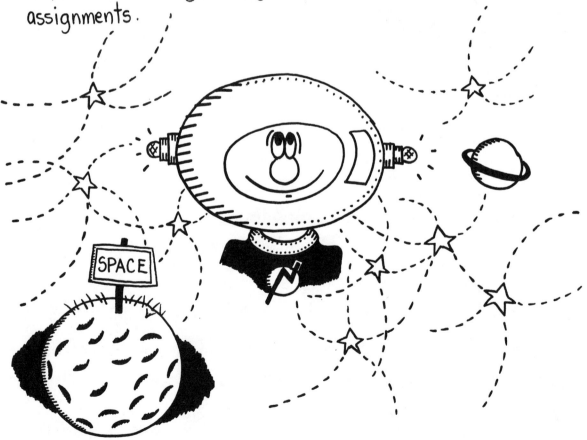

SPACE

questioning "EPICAC"... ♥♥♥

1- Why didn't EPICAC work out the way he was supposed to?

2- Look up the word "vindicate." Why do you think the narrator of the story wants to <u>vindicate</u> EPICAC?

3- Can people ever be like machines in any way? Why or why not?

4- Originally, why didn't Pat want to marry the narrator of the story?

5- How was the narrator "using" EPICAC?

6- If machines are built by people to serve people, which is superior (or smarter)?.. humans for creating the machines or the machines for performing the work better and faster?

7- What was EPICAC's unsolvable problem?

8- Who was more "human" in the end, EPICAC or the man? Define what you mean by "human".

9- For <u>EPICAC</u>, was it better to have loved and lost than to have <u>never</u> loved at all?

10- Was the narrator a murderer or did the machine commit suicide?

11- What kind of person was the narrator?

12- What does the last line mean - "Say nothing but good of the dead?" Why do you think the author ended the story this way? Did the narrator have any right to say anything bad about EPICAC?

13- How is this story <u>science fiction</u>? Explain.

2 poems...

① Atomic Courtesy

To smash the simple atom
All mankind was intent
Now any day the atom...
May return the compliment!

                    — ETHEL JACOBSON

② Earth

"A planet doesn't explode of itself," said drily
The Martian astronomer, gazing off into the air —
"That they were able to do it is proof that highly
Intelligent beings must have been living there."

                    — JOHN HALL WHEELOCK

1 How are these two poems being <u>SARCASTIC</u>? *LOOK UP THIS WORD*

2 What is the author's <u>prediction</u> for mankind in poem #1?

3 How is poem #2 a <u>CONTRADICTION</u>? *LOOK UP THIS WORD*

4 Poem #2 implies that "intelligence" isn't always put to the best use. If you think this is true, prove it by using <u>specific</u> examples. If you think this is false, give your reasons why.

5 Are these poems "science <u>fiction</u>", <u>or</u> is there any truth in them? Why or why not?

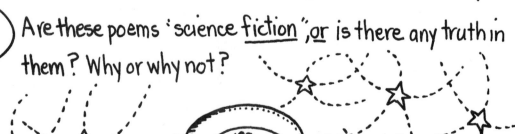

fiction ...or fact?

KNOCK!

...a man sits in his chair after the total destruction of the world—he knows that all other humans have been destroyed. There is a knock at the door... who is it? Or, what is it?

...November 4, 2976. The first robot has been elected President of the World...

...Macy's Department Store announced a sale today on their huge stock of mechanical pets, rumored to be just like the "real thing." Of course, nobody has seen the "real thing" for over 2000 years...

...It is the year 2500. Government scientists are making their last desperate effort to save the <u>only</u> flower in the country...

Choose <u>one</u> of the above topics and develop it into a six paragraph story. Be sure to include setting, character development (human or <u>non</u>-human), events leading up to the story, the problem, the solution, what happened, how it happened, and why it happened. Allow your imagination to take over.

Space Spelling...

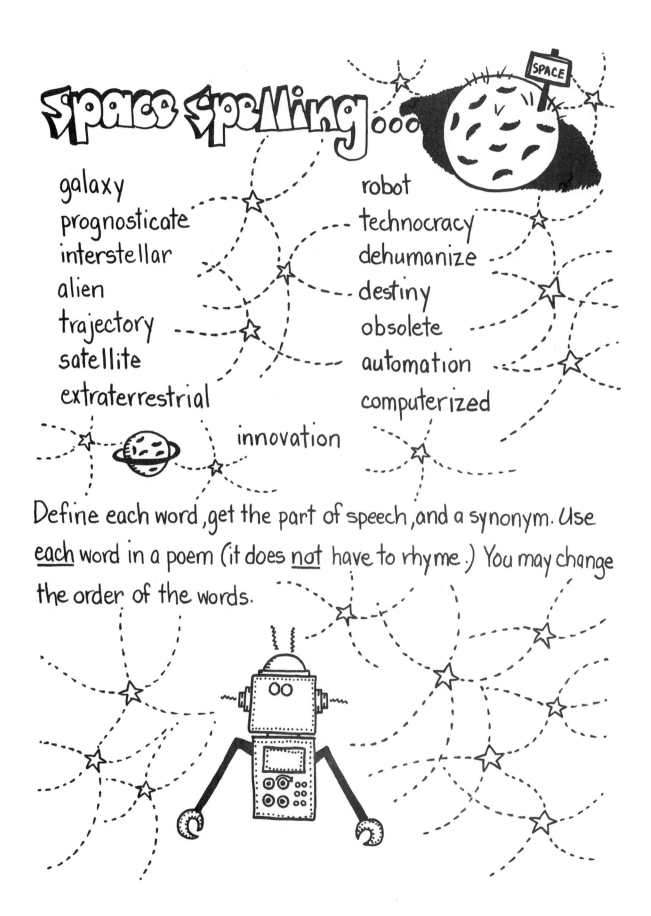

galaxy

prognosticate

interstellar

alien

trajectory

satellite

extraterrestrial

innovation

robot

technocracy

dehumanize

destiny

obsolete

automation

computerized

Define each word, get the part of speech, and a synonym. Use _each_ word in a poem (it does _not_ have to rhyme.) You may change the order of the words.

Loneliness:

Richard Cory
Eleanor Rigby
Too Blue
A Coney Island Life

Richard Cory

Edwin Arlington Robinson

Whenever Richard Cory went down town,
We people on the pavement looked at him:
He was a gentleman from sole to crown,
Clean favored, and imperially slim.

And he was always quietly arrayed,
And he was always human when he talked;
But still he fluttered pulses when he said,
"Good morning," and he glittered .when he walked.

And he was rich—yes, richer than a king—
And admirably schooled in every grace:
In fine, we thought that he was everything
To make us wish that we were in his place.

So on we worked, and waited for the light,
And went without the meat, and cursed the bread;
And Richard Cory, one calm summer night,
Went home and put a bullet through his head.

1- Describe the kind of person talking in this poem.

2- What did the people think of Richard Cory?

3- Things aren't always what they appear to be. How does this statement apply to this poem?

4- Is there any evidence in this poem that suggests that Richard Cory took his life because he was a lonely man? If so, what? If not, why do you think he took his life?

5- Can commiting suicide ever be a positive act (a good thing?) Why or why not?

6- How is suicide the dirtiest trick anyone can play?

7- Who do you think was better off in this poem, Richard Cory or the people? (Remember, even though Mr. Cory ended up dead, the people were obviously very poor, worked extremely hard, and were jealous, as a whole.)

8- Do you think the people had any reasons to envy Richard Cory?

9- How important are appearances?

10- What does envy or jealousy do to people and why does it occur?

Eleanor Rigby

John Lennon & Paul McCartney

Ah—look at all the lonely people!
Eleanor Rigby, picks up the rice in the church where a wedding has been, lives in a dream.
Waits at the window, wearing the face that she keeps in a jar by the door, who is it for?
All the lonely people, where do they all come from?
All the lonely people, where do they all belong?

Father McKenzie, writing the words of a sermon that no one will hear, no one comes near.
Look at him working, darning his socks in the night when there's nobody there, what does he care?
All the lonely people, where do they all come from?
All the lonely people, where do they all belong?

Eleanor Rigby, died in the church and was buried along with her name, nobody came.
Father McKenzie, wiping the dirt from his hands as he walks from the grave, no one was saved.
All the lonely people, where do they all come from?
All the lonely people, where do they all belong?

1- What do Eleanor Rigby and Father McKenzie have in common?

2- Why do you think Eleanor Rigby has another face?

3- What "masks" do you wear? Be specific. Why do people need masks, or do they?

4- How important do you think communication is in any relationship?

5- How important is communication to life? Is not being able to communicate a kind of suicide? Explain.

6- Is it possible that people could be in church but still not hear Father McKenzie's sermons? How could this happen?

7- Why was no one saved? Explain.

8- Can you ever be lonely in a room filled with people? Why or why not?

9- How does "loneliness" differ from "being alone?"

10- "All the lonely people, where do they all belong?"

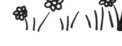

too blue

Langston Hughes

I got those sad old weary blues
I don't know where to turn,
I don't know where to go, Nobody cares about you
When you sink so low.

What shall I do?
What shall I say?
Shall I take a gun and
Put myself away?

I wonder if
One bullet would do?
Hard as my head is,
It would probably take two.

But I ain't got
Neither bullet nor gun—
And I'm too blue
To look for one.

1- What kind of mood do you think the narrator of this poem is in?

2- What action is the narrator considering?

3- The person in this poem is going through a kind of "paralysis" (he can't decide whether or not to take his life.) Is this indecision, or paralysis, itself, a kind of suicide?

4- "Choosing is existence (life or living.) If you don't choose, you don't exist." Do you agree with this? Why or why not?

5- What does this person mean when he says he has a "hard head?"

6- It is probably true that one bullet in the head would kill a person, so why does the narrator say he would probably need two?

7- Do you agree with this statement: "If you <u>want</u> to live, you <u>should</u> live, if you <u>want</u> to die, you <u>should</u> die." Why or why not?

8- Why do you think that in this country suicide is considered a crime?

9- Why do you think people (or you) get depressed? Explain.

a coney island life

James L. Weil

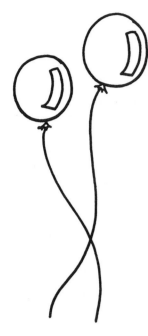

Having lived a Coney Island life
on rollercoaster ups and downs
and seen my helium hopes
break skyward without me,
now arms filled with dolls
I threw so much for
I take perhaps my last ride
on this planet-carousel
and ask
how many more times round
I have
to catch that brass-ring-sun
before the game is up.

1- Describe the kind of person talking in the poem.

2- What are some of the ups and downs in <u>your</u> life ?

3- What is "the game" the poet is talking about in the last line ?

4- How is life like a game ?

5- How do you feel about the proverb: "If you don't succeed at first, try, try again ?" Should you always try again ? Is there ever a time when you should quit ? Explain your answers.

6- Do you believe that <u>everything</u> in life happens for the best ? Why or why not ?

Sometimes i wonder:

Tapestry
Garbage
What Am I Doing Here?
Old Friends
The Term

tapestry

Don McLean

Every thread of creation is held in position
By still other strands of things living
In an earthly tapestry hung from the skyline of smoldering cities
So gray and so vulgar as not to be satisfied with their own negativity
But needing to touch all the living as well.

Every breeze that blows kindly is one crystal breath
We exhale on the blue diamond heaven
As gentle to touch as the hands of the healer
As soft as farewells whispered over the coffin
We're poisoned with venom with each breath we take
From the brown sulphur chimney
And the black highway snake.

Every dawn that breaks golden is held in suspension
Like the yolk of the egg in albumen
Where the birth and the death of unseen generations
Are interdependent in vast orchestration
And painted in colors of tapestry thread
When the dying are born and the living are dead.

Every pulse of your heartbeat is one liquid moment
That flows through the veins of your being
Like a river of life flowing on since creation
Approaching the sea with each new generation
You're now just a stagnant and rancid disgrace
That is rapidly drowning the whole human race.
Every fish that swims silent, every bird that flies freely
Every doe that steps softly
Every crisp leave that falls, all the flowers that grow
On this colorful tapestry, somehow they know
That if man is allowed to destroy all we need
He will soon have to pay with his life
For his greed.

tapestry

1- What is a tapestry?

2- Why do you think the title of this poem is "Tapestry?"

3- This poem talks about the chain of life -do you agree that everything in this world, the past, present, and future, is linked together by the thread of life? Why or why not?

4- <u>Who</u> and <u>what</u> are <u>you</u> dependent on?

5- What does the poet mean when he says that every dawn (or day) is "held in suspension?"

6- Why do you think the poet compared life to a vast orchestra?

7- What is happening to the world, according to the poet?

8- Why does the poet call human beings "greedy?"

9- What does this line mean: "When the dying are born and the living are dead?"

10- How do you think the poet feels about the <u>quality</u> of life on earth? How do <u>you</u> feel about it?

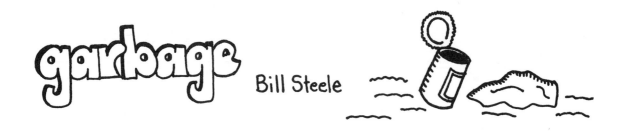

garbage

Bill Steele

Mister Thompson calls the waiter, orders steak and baked potato
But he leaves the bone and gristle and he never eats the skins;
Then the bus boy comes and takes it, with a cough contaminates it
As he puts it in a can with coffee grounds and sardine tins;
The the truck comes by on Friday and carts it all away;
And a thousand trucks just like it are converging on the bay.
Garbage!!! Garbage!!! We're filling up the sea with garbage.
Garbage!!! Garbage!!!
What will we do when there's no place left to put all the garbage?

Mister Thompson starts his Cadillac and winds it up the freeway track
Leaving friends and neighbors in a hydrocarbon haze
He's joined by lots of smaller cars all sending gases to the stars
There to form a seething cloud that hangs for thirty days
While the sun licks down upon it with its ultraviolet tongues
'Til it turns to smog and settles down and ends up in our lungs.
Garbage!!! Garbage!!! We're filling up the sky with garbage.
Garbage!!! Garbage!!!
What will we do when there's nothing left to breathe but garbage?

Getting home and taking off his shoes he settles down with evening news
While the kids do homework with the T.V. in one ear
While Superman for thousandth time sells talking dolls and conquers crime
They dutifully learn the date of birth of Paul Revere
In the paper there's a piece about the mayor's middle name,
And he gets it done in time to watch the All-Star Bingo Game
Garbage!!! Garbage!!! We're filling up our minds with garbage!
Garbage!!! Garbage!!!
What will we do when there's nothing left to read
and there's nothing left to hear and there's nothing left to need
and there's nothing left to wear and there's nothing left to talk about
and nothing left to walk upon and nothing left to care about
and nothing left to ponder on and nothing left to touch
and there's nothing left to see and there's nothing left to do
and there's nothing left to be—but garbage?

164

garbage

1- This poem is about different types of garbage—what is garbage?

2- What is the message the poet is trying to get across?

3- It has been said that the mind is a junkyard—do you agree, why or why not?

4- What kinds of garbage do you fill your mind with?

5- What would life be like when there's "nothing left to walk upon, or care about, or see, or touch, or do?" How important are these things for life?

6- Can a person ever become "garbage?" Why or why not?

7- If there's nothing left to be (last line), what options are open to you? Do you have any options? Are options important in living?

what am i doin' here?

Ric Masten

When you're takin' that vacation
Out in the countryside
Don't stay too long there in the wilderness
'Cause a man seems kinda small
And a mountain awful tall
It could make you look inside yourself and ask . . .
Where did I come from
Where am I goin'
And what am I doin' here.

When you're drivin' in the country
Keep a-steppin' on the gas
Hurry, hurry, hurry on your way
If ya slow down to a walk
Ya might hear the country talk
You might hear the country laugh and say . . .
Where did you come from
Where are you goin'
And what are you doin' here.

Keep the radio playin'
And turn the volume up
Keep your transistor plugged into your ear
If you listen and you're still
In the silence of the hills
Ya might hear things you didn't want to hear . . .
Like: where did ya' come from
Where are ya goin'
And what are you doin' here.

what am i doin' here ?

Leave your litter in the forest
And scattered by the road
So man can feel a little more at home
The telltale signs of man
His paper and his cans
We see 'em and we think we're not alone . . .
But where did we come from
Where are we goin'
And what are we doin' here.

Are we gonna keep a-runnin'
From the questions that we fear
Until we bring the whole thing crashin' down
And on the day we disappear
There'll be no one left to hear
The burnin' sky ask the barren ground
Where did they come from
And where were they goin'
And what . . .
Were they doin' here?

1- What kinds of things do you miss by rushing through life?

2- How is the poet being <u>sarcastic</u> in this poem?

3- What is the poet's prophecy for the future?

4- It has been said that sometimes you look at things and don't really see them, and that you listen to things but don't really hear them. Explain how this might be true.

5- Why is it important to ask yourself questions?

6- Why wouldn't you want to hear the questions asked in this poem? Or would you?

7- What kinds of things might <u>you not</u> want to hear about yourself and the world you are living in?

8- Where did <u>you</u> come from, where are <u>you</u> going, and what are you doing here?

Old Friends

Paul Simon

Old friends,
Old friends
Sat on their park bench
Like bookends.

A newspaper blown through the grass
Falls on the round toes
On the high shoes
Of the old friends.

Old friends,
Winter companions,
The old men
Lost in their overcoats,
Waiting for the sunset.
The sounds of the city,
Sifting through trees,
Settle like dust
On the shoulders
Of the old friends.

Can you imagine us
Years from today,
Sharing a park bench quietly?
How terribly strange
To be seventy.

Old friends,
Memory brushes the same years.
Silently sharing the same fear . . .

Old Friends

1- Why do <u>you</u> think the people were compared to bookends?

2- Why are the men waiting for the sunset?

3- Why do you think they were sitting on the bench all day?

4- What do you think are the patterns in these people's lives?

5- How do <u>you</u> feel about growing old?

6- What is the fear that these people share?

7- Why do you think some people fear getting old?

8- Is it ever possible to have too much time? Why or why not?

9- What do you think about the fact that when you finally have so much time to do whatever you want (due to retirement etc.), you have so little time left to live?

10- How should people "wait for the end" – or should they wait at all?

11- Compare the seasons of the year (spring, summer, fall, and winter) to growing old.

The Term

William Carlos Williams

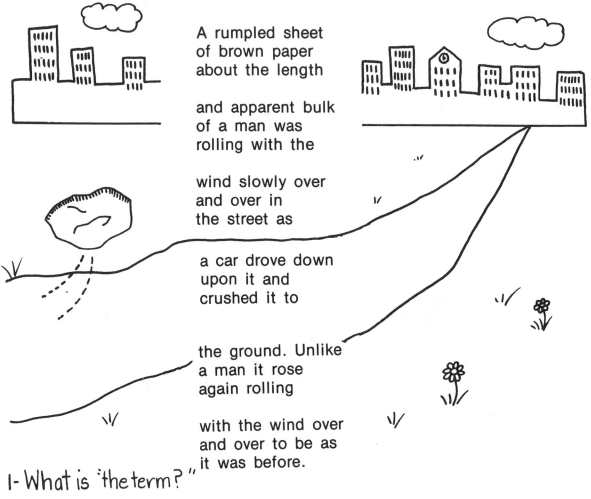

A rumpled sheet
of brown paper
about the length

and apparent bulk
of a man was
rolling with the

wind slowly over
and over in
the street as

a car drove down
upon it and
crushed it to

the ground. Unlike
a man it rose
again rolling

with the wind over
and over to be as
it was before.

1- What is "the term?"

2- The paper rose again after it was crushed, what does this suggest to you?

3- Things live forever (or a lot longer than people.) People die. Could this be a
    message as to what or who is really important in the scheme of life?

4- Humans have searched for ways to become <u>immortal</u> - is immortality important to <u>you</u>?

5- How important is the life of anyone or anything, if all things eventually die?

6- How are people <u>vulnerable</u> - are other living things more <u>or</u> less vulnerable than humans?

7- What are the <u>patterns</u> that are talked about in this poem?

how do i fit? 8

Do I fit?

Southbound on the Freeway

May Swenson

A tourist came in from Orbitville,
parked in the air, and said: The creatures of this star
are made of metal and glass.
Through the transparent parts
you can see their guts.
Their feet are round and roll
on diagrams or long
measuring tapes, dark
with white lines.
They have four eyes
The two in back are red.
Sometimes you can see a five-eyed
one, with a red eye turning
on the top of his head.
He must be special—
the others respect him
and go slow
when he passes, winding
among them from behind.
They all hiss as they glide,
like inches, down the marked
tapes. Those soft shapes,
shadowy inside
the hard bodies—are they
their guts or their brains?

Southbound on the Freeway

1- According to the tourist, who inhabits the earth?

2- What are the diagrams that the poet talks about?

3- What is the five-eyed creature with the red eye?

4- What are the soft shapes that are inside the hard bodies?

5- From what you have just read, how do you think this poet looks at life?

6- What does this poem say about <u>technology</u>?

7- Do you think this is an accurate picture of what life is like today? Why or why not?

8- Do you think there is any truth in what the tourist sees? Why or why not?

9- Why do you think the poet chose to call the poem "Southbound on the <u>Freeway</u>", rather than "Southbound on the Highway", or "Interstate," or "Thruway," or "Parkway"..? (Hint: Look carefully at the word "Freeway.")

10- Answer the question at the end of the poem. In other words, do people control machines or do machines control people? <u>WHY</u>?

The Forecast

Dan Jaffe

Perhaps our age has driven us indoors.
We sprawl in the semi-darkness, dreaming sometimes
Of a vague world spinning in the wind.
But we have snapped our locks, pulled down our shades,
Taken all precautions. We shall not be disturbed.
If the earth shakes, it will be on a screen;
And if the prairie wind spills down our streets
And covers us with leaves, the weatherman will tell us.

1- Why do you think this poem is called "The Forecast?"

2- What does the poet predict will happen to humans in the future?

3- Considering life as it is now, and might be, why do you think people might be driven indoors?

4- According to the poet, _how_ will people feel things, sense things, know things, and learn things?

5- Is this forecast optimistic? Why or why not?

6- Do you ever feel like shutting yourself off from the rest of the world? Why or why not?

7- One idea that can be gotten from the poem is that people are losing touch with the "real" world (reality.) _Why_ and _how_ could this happen?

8- What can _you_ do to keep in touch with the "real" world?

9- Is looking at the world (life) through machines (television, movies, etc.) real or unreal? _Why_?

 **Paul Simon**

The night set softly
With the hush of falling leaves
Casting shivering shadows
On the houses through the trees
And light from a street lamp
Paints a pattern on my wall
Like the pieces of a puzzle
Or a child's uneven scrawl.

Up a narrow flight of stairs
In a narrow little room
As I lie upon my bed
In the early evening gloom.
Impaled on my wall
My eyes can dimly see
The patterns of my life
And the puzzle that is me.

From the moment of my birth
To the instant of my death
There are patterns I must follow
Just as I must breathe each breath.
Like a rat in a maze
The path before me lies
And the pattern never alters
Until the rat dies

And the pattern still remains
On the wall where darkness fell
And it's fitting that it should
For in darkness I must dwell.
Like the color of my skin
Or the day that I grow old
My life is made of patterns
That can scarcely be controlled.

1. What is a pattern?

2. What are some of the patterns <u>you must</u> follow?

3. Why do you think the poet calls himself a puzzle?

4. How is a puzzle like a pattern?

5. What type of person do you think would write a poem like this?

6. What is the poet saying about life?

7. Describe a person who you know. Tell what patterns s/he fits into and <u>why</u> you think that person has chosen those patterns.

8. Do <u>you</u> always choose your patterns? Why or why not?

9. Can you do anything to alter (change) the pattern of your life? If so, what?

10. How do patterns determine your fate and fortune?

11. For what do we use patterns?

175

the circle game

Joni Mitchell

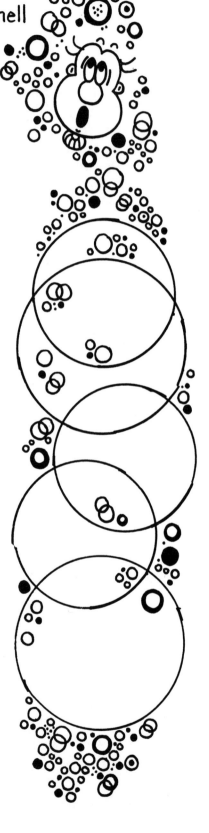

Yesterday a child came out to wonder
Caught a dragonfly inside a jar
Fearful when the sky was full of thunder
And tearful at the falling of a star
Then the child moved ten times round the seasons
Skated over ten clear frozen streams
Words like, when you're older, must appease him
And promises of someday make his dreams

    And the seasons they go round and round
    And the painted ponies go up and down
    We're captive on the carousel of time
    We can't return, we can only look behind
    From where we came
    And go round and round and round
    In the circle game

Sixteen springs and sixteen summers gone now
Cartwheels turn to car wheels thru the town
And they tell him, Take your time, it won't be long now
Till you drag your feet to slow the circles down

    And the seasons they go round and round
    And the painted ponies go up and down
    We're captive on the carousel of time
    We can't return, we can only look behind
    From where we came
    And go round and round and round
    In the circle game.

So the years spin by and now the boy is twenty
Though his dreams have lost some grandeur coming true
There'll be new dreams, maybe better dreams and plenty
Before the last revolving year is through.

    And the seasons they go round and round
    And the painted ponies go up and down
    We're captive on the carousel of time
    We can't return, we can only look behind
    From where we came
    And go round and round and round
    In the circle game.

The circle game

1- How is life like being on a carousel?

2- Why do you think this poem is called "The Circle Game?"

3- What can't you return to? (see line #12.)

4- How can <u>time</u> hold you captive?

5- How is the passing of time (the circle game) like a pattern?

6- How do you think the poet feels about the past?

7- Why do people want to "slow the circles down?"

8- What happens to people's <u>lives</u> and <u>feelings</u> once they start playing the circle game?

9- How do <u>you</u> play the circle game?

10- It has been said that we look at the present through a rear-view mirror (think of being in a car.) In other words, we are a nation that marches backwards into the future. Do <u>you</u> think the ideas in this poem agree or disagree with this statement? Why or why not?

11- Can you ever stop playing the circle game? If so, when? Or, why not?

12- How do <u>you</u> <u>feel</u> about the circle game?

little boxes

Malvina Reynolds

Little boxes on the hillside,
Little boxes made of ticky tacky,
Little boxes on the hillside,
Little boxes all the same.
There's a green one and a pink one
And a blue one and a yellow one
And they're all made out of ticky tacky
And they all look just the same.

And the people in the houses
All went to the university,
Where they were put in boxes
And they came out all the same,
And there's doctors and lawyers,
And business executives
And they're all made out of ticky tacky
And they all look just the same.

And they all play on the golf course
And drink their martinis dry,
And they all have pretty children
And the children go to school,
And the children go to summer camp
And then to the university,
Where they are put in boxes
And they come out all the same.

And the boys go into business
And marry and raise a family
In boxes made of ticky tacky
And they all look just the same.
There's a green one and a pink one,
And a blue one and a yellow one,
And they're all made out of ticky tacky
And they all look just the same.

178

little boxes

1- What are the little boxes on the hillside?

2- How is this poem's message like the one in the "Circle Game?"

3- Does the poet think people's lives fit into patterns? Why?

4- What kinds of boxes are people put into during their lives? List some. (The poem mentions several...)

5- "Ticky tacky" is a nonsense word, it has <u>no</u> real meaning. Why do <u>you</u> think the poet used this word over and over again in the poem?

6- How can the people in the poem be compared to an assembly line in a factory?

7- What do <u>you</u> think is missing from these people's lives, if anything?

8- How important do you think it is to be an individual? Why?

9- Why do you think a lot of people are comfortable or happy with their little boxes?

10- Are there any little boxes in your life? If so, what are they? If not, explain why.

the poet in you...

You will write five poems (a minimum of <u>ten</u> lines each.) The topics for the poems can be chosen from the following:

1-How you feel about yourself.

2-How you see other people.

3-The part of the city or town you live in that is you.

4-How you fit into your family.

5-How school affects you.

6-The patterns in your life.

7-The patterns of your life in <u>ten</u> years. (Think of how old you will be and what you are likely to be doing.)

The poems do not have to rhyme. It is more important that they be thought out and express your feelings.

follow your star : 8

- Where Do I Go ?
- If I Had Wings
- Spelling Assignment
- Mirror Writing
- For Two Cents
- Insight

where do i go?

from the musical <u>Hair</u>

"Where do I go? Follow the River. Where do I go?
Follow the Gull. Where is the something? Where is the someone? That tells me why I live and die.
Where do I go? Follow the children. Where do I go?
Follow their smiles. Is there an answer in their sweet faces
That tells me why I live and die?
Follow the wind. Follow the thunder
Follow the neon in young lover's eyes
Down to the gutter, up to the glitter
Into the city where the truth lies
Where do I go? Follow my heartbeat. Where do I go? Follow my hand.
Where will they lead me and will I ever discover why I live and die?
Why do I live? Why do I die? Tell me where do I go
Tell me why
Tell me where
Tell me why
Tell me where
Tell me why!"

1- Is it important to know where you are going in life? Why or why not?

2- Do you think it's better to automatically get what you want in life <u>or</u> to work for it?

3- Does meeting challenges help or hurt you in life? Why?

4- What kinds of things do <u>you</u> follow in your life? <u>Why</u> do you follow them?

5- Do you let yourself be led or do you lead yourself?

6- Do you think people ever discover why they live and die?

7- Answer these questions as they apply to <u>you</u>: Where do I go? Who will lead me? How would life be different without me?

8- This song asks a lot of questions and answers very few. What questions do you ask yourself that are still unanswered? List at least three questions like this. Why do think you still <u>don't</u> have the answers?

if i had wings

Peter Yarrow and Susan Yardley

If I had wings no one would ask me should I fly
The birds sing, no one asks why.
I can see in myself wings as I feel them
If you see something else keep your thoughts to yourself
I'll fly free then.

Yesterday's eyes see their colors fading away
They see their sun turning to grey
You can't share in a dream that you don't believe in
If you say that you see and pretend to be me
You won't be then.

How can you ask if I'm happy goin' my way?
You might as well ask a child at play!
There is no need to discuss or understand me
I won't ask of myself to become something else
I'll just be me!

If I had wings no one would ask me should I fly
The birds sing, no one asks why.
I can see in myself wings as I feel them
If you see something else keep your thoughts to yourself
I'll fly free then.

1- Do people's opinions of you hold you back from doing things? Why or why not?

2- Do you have difficulty being different from your friends? Why or why not?

3- Do you think that people who go their own way are happy?

4- Why do you think the person in the song says, "There is no need to discuss or understand me"...do you ever feel that way? Why or why not?

5- Is "I did it my way" always the best thing to do?

6- Summarize this song, explaining what each stanza means to you.

mirror writing...

1. "Grown up, and that is a terribly hard thing to do. It is much easier to skip it and go from one childhood to another." —F. SCOTT FITZGERALD

2. "It is unjust to claim the privileges of age, and retain the playthings of childhood." — SAMUEL JOHNSON

3. "To be adult is to be alone." —JEAN ROSTAND

4. "The turning point in the process of growing up is when you discover the core of strength within you that survives all hurt." —MAX LERNER

5. "The strongest principle of growth lies in human choice." —GEORGE ELIOT

6. "He who would learn to fly one day must first learn to stand and walk and run and climb and dance: one cannot fly into flying." —NIETZSCHE

CHOOSE ANY <u>THREE</u> OF THE ABOVE QUOTATIONS :

Paragraph #1... Explain its meaning in detail.

Paragraph #2... How does this quotation apply to you?

Paragraph #3... Explain the quotation in terms of id, ego, and super-ego.

Do each of the above for all <u>3</u> quotations you pick. You will have a total of <u>9</u> paragraphs.

<u>Teacher</u>: This was done after a discussion of id, ego, and super-ego.

Spelling

...Find the definition, part of speech, and a synonym for each word. Then, write an <u>EXAMPLE</u> for each word. Have your examples deal with some part of your personality, growing up, or your relationship with other people.

1. stereotype	5. expectation	9. identity	13. pressure
2. rapport	6. peer	10. disillusion	14. consequence
3. tradition	7. conformity	11. heritage	15. prejudice
4. unique	8. sacrifice	12. maturity	16. uncertainty

for 2¢...

The human being is made up of oxygen, nitrogen, phosphorous, hydrogen, carbon, and calcium. There are also 12½ gallons of water, enough iron to make a small nail, about a salt-shaker full of salt, and enough sugar to make one small cube. If one were to put all of this together and try to sell it, the whole thing would be worth about one dollar.

1. What do you think is the point of this statement?

2. In what ways are you worth more than $1.00?

3. What are some ways we measure the worth of human beings?

4. How important is the money value of a thing?

insight ooo Answer these questions:

1. How often do you consider the consequences of what you do <u>before</u> acting?

2. How do you <u>know</u> when something is wrong or right?

3. Why should some people get paid more than others for working - or should they?

4. How come so many people want to "get ahead" and are never satisfied?

5. When, if at all, is it right to tell on someone? *I wonder...*

6. When, if at all, is it good to take a dare?

7. How often do you do things of which you are <u>not</u> proud?

8. What is one thing you <u>don't</u> want to be when you get older? Why?

9. How often do you do things just because others expect you to do them that way?

10. How often do you hurt people when you really don't mean to?

Many times people only consider <u>one</u> side of an argument. The next four questions ask you to take an <u>unpopular</u> point of view. You don't have to agree with what you write—sometimes it is good to look at "the other side." You might change your mind or you might convince yourself you were right all along.

In one paragraph (or more) for each of the following, <u>defend</u> the point of view that is being represented.

1. What is good about war? (WAR IS GOOD.) *WHAT!*

2. What is good about prejudice? (PREJUDICE IS GOOD.)

3. What is <u>not</u> good about being generous? (BEING GENEROUS IS BAD.)

4. What is <u>not</u> good about being smart? (BEING SMART IS BAD.)

IV. Tools of the trade...

write-on ooo

Okay, you can write (you learned how to do that back in the first grade!) but one of the things that we're after this year is to make your writing interesting to read...

- SOME THINGS TO KEEP IN MIND WHEN YOU WRITE -

1 One of the best ways to improve the quality of your writing is to start thinking about the <u>type</u> of words you choose...some words suggest special <u>moods</u>. Usually, these kinds of words are adjectives. <u>Think</u> before you use a word in a story. Compare these → "The wind blew...", "The wind rattled the empty trees...", "The sun was very hot..." "The blazing sun scorched the earth..." Ask yourself, "Is there a more descriptive way to say it?" Find these words in a thesaurus.

2 Pay attention to <u>details</u>, they can make things come alive.

3 Use <u>specific</u> <u>examples</u>, especially when you are trying to prove a point.

4 Try to answer these questions whenever possible: <u>WHO</u>, <u>WHAT</u>, <u>WHY</u>, <u>WHERE</u>, <u>WHEN</u>, <u>HOW</u>.

5 <u>Describe</u> as much as you can, <u>in detail</u>.

6 If possible, <u>look</u> at things <u>before</u> you write about them...you'll be surprised at how much you can forget - even with familiar things!

7 <u>Feelings</u> make your writing more personal.

8 <u>Always</u> <u>proofread</u> your paper! Whenever you write something, read it over at least <u>one</u> time to be sure it sounds all right and that it makes sense. Then look for spelling and grammatical errors.

perfect paragraphing...

Paragraphs are used in all kinds of writing. A paragraph is a group of sentences (usually 6-8) that talks about and develops <u>one</u> topic.

• The <u>first</u> sentence of a paragraph is called the <u>Topic Sentence</u>. The Topic Sentence tells <u>what</u> the paragraph is going to be about.

• The next few sentences develop (talk about) your topic. The sentences can be many different kinds. They can include facts or specific examples, descriptions, opinions, explanations, or incidents.

• The <u>last</u> sentence of a paragraph is called the <u>Concluding Sentence</u>. This sentence summarizes your paragraph. You can do this by using <u>different</u> words to re-state your Topic Sentence.

-<u>A Sample Paragraph</u>-

Indent

    → Fort River is an elementary school in Amherst, Massachusetts. ←— *Topic Sentence*
The school is a one floor building with classrooms that are called "quads." Each quad has three home corners. Fort River also has a library called the Media Materials Center. The school has two cafeterias and a large gymnasium. The school was built in 1973. Fort River is one of five elementary schools in this town. ←— *CONCLUDING SENTENCE*

the other word

o oo the quality of your writing depends on the <u>words</u> you choose to use. Instead of always using words like "big", "small", "good", "pretty", etc. develop a vocabulary of more interesting adjectives. For the words below, find words that mean the same thing or nearly the same thing, by looking in a dictionary or thesaurus, or thinking of more interesting words yourself! Use this paper when you write.

BIG	SMALL	OLD	YOUNG
1. gigantic	1.	1.	1.
2.	2.	2.	2.
3.	3.	3.	3.
4.	4.	4.	4.

HAPPY	SAD	BEAUTIFUL	SOUR
1.	1.	1.	1.
2.	2.	2.	2.
3.	3.	3.	3.
4.	4.	4.	4.

COLD	RED	GREEN	BLUE
1.	1.	1.	1.
2.	2.	2.	2.
3.	3.	3.	3.
4.	4.	4.	4.

HOT	RICH	FAT	THIN
1.	1.	1.	1.
2.	2.	2.	2.
3.	3.	3.	3.
4.	4.	4.	4.

<u>Teacher</u>: This assignment can be repeated often. By using different words you help your students expand their vocabulary.

First lines

ooo What can you tell about these stories from their first lines?

"It was a bright cold day in April, and the clocks were striking thirteen."
1984

"Crossing the lawn that morning, Douglas Spaulding broke a spider web with his face. A single invisible line on the air touched his brow and snapped without a sound."
Dandelion Wine

"A screaming comes across the sky. It has happened before, but there is nothing to compare it to now."
Gravity's Rainbow

"It was a pleasure to burn. It was special pleasure to see things eaten, to see things blackened and changed."
Fahrenheit 451

"I read about it in the paper, in the subway, on my way to work, I read it and I couldn't believe it, and I read it again."
"Sonny's Blues"

"Alan Austen, as nervous as a kitten, went up certain dark and creaky stairs in the neighborhood of Pell Street and peered about for a long time on the dim landing before he found the name he wanted written obscurely on one of the doors."
"The Chaser"

"During the whole of a dull, dark, and soundless day in the autumn of the year, when the clouds hung oppressively low in the heavens, I had been passing alone, on horseback, through a singularly dreary tract of country, and at length found myself, as the shades of the evening drew on, within view of the melancholy House of Usher."
"The Fall of the House of Usher"

"It was late and every   the shadow the leaves of the tree made

R. J. Bauman, who fo   through Mississippi, drove his F

"It was quite a summe   up, was yellow hot and small as a quarter. T   d outside of town only the early cotton had

[handwritten note: Type "The Fall of the House of Usher" — Double space — Large]

Writ   ? 👀 ?

1. a circus coming to t   first winter snowstorm.
4. an incredibly hot d   aceship landing on the moon.
7. someone who is ab   he or she hasn't studied for.
8. someone who is expecting a bike for Christmas and only sees small boxes under the tree.
9. a person who has to get his or her tooth pulled by a dentist.
10. a child running away from home.

the essay

...the purpose of an essay is to make clear to the reader the idea which the author has chosen as his or her subject, as well as to make the author's attitude about the subject, clear. The author may, at times, try to challenge the reader to examine his or her own opinion of the subject, and perhaps change that opinion. Since most people like to make up their own minds, a person who writes an essay needs to be as convincing as possible. Essays can be written in many different ways. They can be done in the form of a story that has a definite point of view. (This is not as easy as it sounds.) Or, they can be done as a straight forward argument that fully discusses a subject. The more facts and specific examples in your essay, the more convincing your essay will be.

Choose <u>two</u> topics from the list below and write an essay on <u>each</u> one:

Comic Books are Worthless
The Freedoms We <u>Don't</u> Have
Computers are Smarter than People

The Possibility of Atomic War
Should Commercials be Allowed on TV?
Television This Year

Medical Care in this Country Should be Free
The Importance of the Equal Rights Amendment
Should Chemical Preservatives be Allowed in Food?
The Appeal of the Fast-Food Restaurants
Time – Our Most Important Possession
Advantages or Disadvantages of Growing Up in a City

No matter what topic you choose, first form a definite opinion, then <u>RESEARCH</u> your topic to get facts to support your argument. Next, decide what <u>FORM</u> your essay will take so you will be able to get your point across and convince your reader in the best possible way. Each essay should be about five paragraphs long.

description checklist ✓

* Use this list when you write...

character: ✓

height	hand size
weight	foot size
hair color	cleanliness
hair texture	jewelry
hair style	clothing worn
eye color	style
shape of eyes	color
shape of nose	fit (baggy, tight, etc.)
shape of mouth	amount
shape of ears	habits
teeth (crooked, braces, etc.)	type of walk
complexion (color, pimples, etc.)	voice (loud, soft, etc.)
shape of face	general appearance
distinguishing features	personality (shy, friendly, etc.)
glasses (shape and color)	intelligence
birthmarks / freckles	age
fingernails (long, polished, etc.)	speech patterns (stutter, accent, etc.)

description checklist ☑
place: ☑

general shape
height
width
outside appearance
colors
function (job) of the place
things in the place
climate
sounds in the place
smells in the place

temperature
material used (wood, brick, etc.)
arrangement of things
where the place is
what it is near
what it is next to
what it is across from
scenery surrounding it
mood of the place
people in the place (number)

object: ☑

color
shape
size
function
weight
texture
cost

temperature
smell
taste
sound it makes
state of motion
how it works
how many parts it has (list)

description checklist ☑

event: ☑

what action took place
how long did it take
where did it happen
when did it happen
who was there
how did each person participate
under what conditions did it happen
why did it happen
how did it happen
mood of the event (panic, happiness, etc.)
result of the event
what happened before the event
what happened after the event

feeling checklist ☑

love, affection, concern:

admired	adorable	affection	agreeable
altruistic	amiable	benevolent	caring
charitable	comforting	congenial	conscientious
considerate	cooperative	cordial	courteous
dedicated	easy-going	empathetic	fair
faithful	forgiving	friendly	generous
genuine	good-humored	helpful	honest
honorable	humane	interested	just
kind	lenient	loving	mellow
moral	neighborly	obliging	open
optimistic	patient	peaceful	polite
reasonable	receptive	reliable	respectful
responsible	sensitive	sympathetic	tender
thoughtful	tolerant	truthful	trustworthy
understanding	unselfish	warm-hearted	well-meaning

feeling checklist ☑
elation, joy:

amused	at ease	blissful	calm
cheerful	comical	contented	ecstatic
enchanted	enthusiastic	excellent	fantastic
glorious	grand	happy	inspired
jovial	jubilant	magnificent	marvelous
overjoyed	pleasant	proud	serene
splendid	superb	thrilled	tremendous
triumphant	turned on	vivacious	witty

potency:

able	assured	authoritative	bold
brave	capable	confident	courageous
daring	determined	durable	dynamic
effective	energetic	forceful	gallant
hardy	healthy	influential	intense
mighty	powerful	secure	self-confident
self-reliant	skillful	strong	tough

feeling checklist ✓

depression:

abandoned	alienated	alone	awful
battered	blue	burned	crushed
defeated	dejected	desolate	despair
despised	despondent	destroyed	discarded
discouraged	dismal	done for	downcast
downtrodden	dreadful	estranged	excluded
forlorn	forsaken	gloomy	grim
hated	hopeless	horrible	humiliated
hurt	in the dumps	left out	loathed
lonesome	low	miserable	mistreated
moody	obsolete	ostracized	out of sorts
overlooked	pathetic	pitiful	regretful
rejected	reprimanded	rotten	ruined
run down	sad	stranded	unhappy
unloved	washed up	whipped	worthless

feeling checklist ☑

distress:

afflicted	anguished	at the mercy of	awkward
baffled	bewildered	confused	disgusted
displeased	dissatisfied	disturbed	doubtful
futile	grief	helpless	hindered
impatient	imprisoned	lost	offended
pained	perplexed	sickened	skeptical
strained	swamped	tormented	touchy
ungainly	unlucky	unpopular	unsure

fear, anxiety:

afraid	agitated	alarmed	apprehensive
desperate	dread	fidgety	frightened
hesitant	horrified	insecure	intimidated
jealous	jittery	nervous	on edge
overwhelmed	panicky	restless	shaky
tense	terrified	uncomfortable	uneasy

feeling checklist ☑

belittling, criticism, scorn:

abused	branded	censured	deflated
diminished	discredited	disgraced	humiliated
jeered	lampooned	laughed at	libeled
maligned	minimized	mocked	neglected
overlooked	put down	ridiculed	roasted
scorned	slandered	slighted	underestimated

impotency, inadequacy:

anemic	broken	cowardly	crippled
debilitated	defective	deficient	demoralized
disabled	exhausted	feeble	fragile
harmless	helpless	incapable	incompetent
ineffective	inept	inferior	insufficient
meek	paralyzed	powerless	shaken
small	trivial	unable	uncertain
unfit	useless	vulnerable	weak

feeling checklist ☑

anger, hostility, cruelty:

agitated	aggravated	aggressive	annoyed
antagonistic	arrogant	belligerent	bigoted
biting	bloodthirsty	blunt	callous
cold-blooded	combative	cantankerous	contrary
cranky	cross	deadly	discontented
dogmatic	enraged	fierce	furious
gruesome	hard	harsh	hateful
heartless	hideous	hostile	inconsiderate
inhuman	insensitive	intolerable	irritated
malicious	mean	murderous	nasty
obstinate	oppressive	poisonous	prejudiced
reckless	resentful	rude	ruthless
sadistic	savage	severe	spiteful
stern	unfeeling	unmerciful	unruly
vicious	vindictive	violent	wrathful